CROWN FINANCIAL MINISTRIES

BUSINESS
BY THE
BOOK
SMALL GROUP STUDY

LARRY BURKETT ◆ HOWARD DAYTON

STUDENT MANUAL

601 BROAD ST SE
GAINESVILLE GA 30501
1-800-722-1976 / Crown.org

ISBN 1-56427-073-4

September 2004 Edition

CONTENTS

FINANCIAL POLICY

- No one may use affiliation with CROWN FINANCIAL MINISTRIES to promote or influence the sale of any financial products or services.

- If you find the study valuable and want to help make it available to others, you may make a tax-deductible gift to CROWN FINANCIAL MINISTRIES.

WEB SITE

CROWN FINANCIAL MINISTRIES has designed a World Wide Web location as a resource to provide students with up-to-date and detailed financial information. It contains helpful articles, a categorized list of the verses dealing with possessions, links to other useful Web sites, and much more.

Visit the Web site at **Crown.org** for a world of information.

DEDICATION

CROWN FINANCIAL MINISTRIES dedicates the *Business By the Book Small Group Study* to the memory of its cofounder Larry Burkett (1939-2003). Larry was a superb pioneer in helping people learn and apply God's financial principles to their lives and businesses.

ACKNOWLEDGEMENTS

CROWN wishes to express profound gratitude to Marlin and Jeanie Horst, Brian Banks, Steve Campbell, Don DeLozier, Phil Drake, Kent Humphreys, Buck Jacobs, Mike Martin, Dave Rae, Stan Reiff, Pat Secrist, and Marc Smith. This group unselfishly invested their time and insights in helping to develop this study.

To participate in this study, you must complete these three requirements before each meeting.

1. HOMEWORK

Everyone is required to complete the homework in writing. The homework questions are designed to take approximately 15 minutes each day to complete. Space is provided in this manual to answer the homework questions. If a couple is taking the study together, they will each have a manual.

2. SCRIPTURE MEMORY

Everyone memorizes an assigned verse each lesson and then individually recites the verse at the beginning of class.

3. PRAYER

Everyone prays for his or her group members each day.

If for any reason someone does not complete all the requirements for a particular lesson, the leader is not to allow him or her to participate in the discussion. This accountability cultivates faithfulness, and the more faithful a person is, the more benefits he or she will derive from the study.

INTRODUCTION

God's Ways Are Not Our Ways

*"All Scripture is inspired by God and profitable for
teaching, for reproof, for correction, for training in
righteousness; that the man of God may be adequate,
equipped for every good work."*
2 Timothy 3:16-17

Before attending the first class, complete the:
☐ Scripture to Memorize
☐ Homework
☐ Optional: We recommend that you read *Business by the Book* by Larry Burkett.

SCRIPTURE TO MEMORIZE

"All Scripture is inspired by God and profitable for teaching, for reproof, for correction, for training in righteousness; that the man of God may be adequate, equipped for every good work" (2 Timothy 3:16-17).

HOMEWORK

Read Isaiah 55:8-9. *"'My thoughts are not your thoughts, nor are your ways My ways,' declares the Lord. 'For as the heavens are higher than the earth, so are My ways higher than your ways, and My thoughts than your thoughts.'"*

1. Based on this passage, do you think that God's business principles will differ from those used by most people to operate a business? In what ways?

2. What are the three biggest challenges you are facing in your business?

   ▪

   ▪

   ▪

3. What do want to learn from this study?

Early one morning, Will, the owner of a large manufacturing company, was greeted at his office door by his plant manager, John. Without comment, John submitted his resignation, effective immediately. Will was devastated; for the past five years he had been grooming John to become president of the company.

When he questioned John about his reasons for leaving, John refused to discuss it. Will could not understand why John was leaving. He was paid more than anyone else in the company, including Will. It was obvious that nothing was going to change John's mind.

Will asked John to stay long enough to hire and train a new plant manager, but he flatly refused and reacted angrily when Will asked. Since John had been such a good friend, Will held a company going-away party and gave John a substantial severance bonus.

Three months later, John's reasons for leaving became apparent: He opened his own company and copied Will's best-selling product. In time, John's company grew, and it became Will's leading competitor.

Nine years later, Will learned there was a design problem with one of John's new products and that several lawsuits were being filed against John's company. Will had forgiven John years before and prayed regularly for him.

He felt strongly that the Lord wanted him to reach out to John, so he bought one of John's products, tested it, and discovered the problem. Then he told his engineers to find a way to fix it. After making and testing the necessary modifications, Will called John and told him how to solve his problem.

Radical Christianity! That's what some would say. Stupidity! That's what others would say.

Only time will tell how John will respond to this act of unconditional Christlike love. The results are not Will's responsibility. His responsibility, like ours, is to do what the Lord wants him to do.

By now you may be thinking: *Where did Will learn to operate his business? Has he lost his mind? What about the bottom line?* But Will's radically different decisions are based on the principles found in the bestselling book of all time—the Bible.

Radical Christianity! That's what some would say. Stupidity! That's what others would say.

Life really didn't change that much between the time Jesus Christ walked the earth and the mid-1800s. People plowed with farm animals, lit their houses with oil lamps, communicated by writing letters, and used horses as the primary means of transportation. The majority of people lived in rural settings.

The business world didn't change that much either. Landowners and tenant farmers herded animals and grew crops. Merchants traded goods in the marketplace. Sales and marketing were local or regional endeavors. Manufacturing was, for the most part, a cottage industry. Businesses were sole proprietorships.

Two developments converged to change everything: new technology with the invention of various kinds of machinery and the emergence of large-scale, capital-raising institutions (banks and the stock market). This convergence, called the Industrial Revolution, made the world of business a very different place.

The years that followed gave rise to big business, industrial monopolies, labor unions, banking, and the first corporate millionaires. Since then, several other economic and technical revolutions have created a business world that would have been unimaginable even 60 years ago. Today, communication and information are instant, competition is global, and governmental regulations are on the rise.

This changing business environment has been accompanied by a change in the way business success is taught. Nineteenth-century business school textbooks were filled with values and principles consistent with the Bible. Success was the product of one's character—integrity, hard work, courage, and the Golden Rule. In the last 50 years, however, the dominant theme is how to increase the bottom line.

Being in business has always been challenging. However, today the difficulty of owning or managing a business by biblical principles is compounded by three realities:

- Most Christians today are far less biblically oriented in their thinking.
- Society is much more secularized.
- The business environment is far more complex.

Because the business environment has become so secular, many Christian businesspeople have responded by going to one of two extremes: either they make no attempt to bring their faith into their workplaces or they conclude that in order to really serve God, they must leave the business world. Many dream of serving God one day when they are able to quit their jobs or sell their businesses. Although God does call some people out of business, He calls most to serve Him in business, where they can influence their customers, vendors, employees, and competitors for Christ.

Nineteenth-century business school textbooks were filled with values and principles consistent with the Bible.

Biblical principles of business often conflict with today's conventional business practices. *"'My thoughts are not your thoughts, nor are your ways My ways,' declares the Lord. 'For as the heavens are higher than the earth, so are My ways higher than your ways, and My thoughts than your thoughts'"* (Isaiah 55:8-9).

Regardless of how different God's thoughts and ways seem to be, the Word of God is as applicable to business today as it has ever been. Isaiah 40:8 reads, *"The grass withers, the flower fades, but the word of our God stands forever."*

OBJECTIVES

This *Business by the Book Small Group Study* is designed to help you, as a business leader, to achieve the following three objectives:

1. To integrate principles from Scripture with your daily business practices

God realizes that business plays a big part in your life. You spend much of your time and energy at work. The Lord knew that your business would be a challenge and even a source of conflict at times.

Because the Lord loves and cares for you deeply, He wanted to prepare you for business. Therefore, God graciously provided His business principles in the Bible. They are a roadmap to guide you in making wise decisions—from hiring and firing to business organization and management.

2. To grow your company profitably

Do the biblical principles of business actually work? Without question they do. However, doing business God's way is not a shortcut to more profits and fewer difficulties. If you implement biblical principles into your business, from time to time it may cost you money. For example, dishonesty is common, and anyone operating a business in a manner that glorifies Christ will face the challenge to compromise or lose money.

Nevertheless, profitability is an essential part of running a business. Christians need to reject the idea that there is something wrong with honestly making money. Isaiah 48:17 says, *"I am the Lord your God, who teaches you to profit, who leads you in the way you should go."* And Psalms 35:27 declares, *"The Lord be magnified, who delights in the prosperity of His servant."* Since the Lord "teaches you to profit," one of the objectives is to help you learn how to operate your business in a way that is both profitable and glorifies to God.

3. To develop leadership skills and to grow in Christ so that you will be more like Him as a business leader

Our Lord Jesus Christ is the most powerful model of leadership in history. Becoming more like Him will enable you to be more effective in every part of your life—as a person, a spouse, a parent, a neighbor—and as a business leader.

Biblical principles of business often conflict with today's conventional business practices. "'My thoughts are not your thoughts, nor are your ways My ways,' declares the Lord. 'For as the heavens are higher than the earth, so are My ways higher than your ways, and My thoughts than your thoughts'" (Isaiah 55:8-9).

INTRODUCTION NOTES

9

Implementing God's principles for operating a business is a journey that takes time. Those who have preceded you in this study have found it to be enormously helpful to them. But it is only the beginning of the journey. It is our hope that you will become involved in a small group of your peers after you complete this study. Such a group can encourage and counsel each other as they study God's business principles in more detail and discover how to apply them to real-life situations.

Some of you are now facing business difficulties. It is important to realize that there is hope! Don't let a sense of guilt over past mistakes overwhelm you; rather, learn from the experience. The Apostle Paul said it this way, *"Forgetting what lies behind and reaching forward to what lies ahead, I press on toward the goal . . ."* (Philippians 3:13-14).

The principles you will learn here are a gift from a loving God intended to benefit you spiritually and practically.

OWNERSHIP and PURPOSE

The Lord Is Owner of All

"Everything in the heavens and earth is yours, O Lord."
1 Chronicles 29:11, TLB

OWNERSHIP and PURPOSE HOMEWORK

Homework to be completed for Chapter 2

Before attending class, complete the:
☐ Scripture to Memorize
☐ Ownership and Purpose Homework
☐ Quit Claim Deed
☐ Optional: Read Chapters 1-3 in *Business by the Book* by Larry Burkett.

SCRIPTURE TO MEMORIZE

"Everything in the heavens and earth is yours, O Lord, and this is your kingdom. We adore you as being in control of everything. Riches and honor come from you alone, and you are the Ruler of all mankind; your hand controls power and might, and it is at your discretion that men are made great and given strength" (1 Chronicles 29:11-12, TLB).

DAY ONE – REVIEW CHAPTER 1

Read the Introduction Notes on pages 7-10 and answer.

1. What information especially impacted you?

2. How will you apply this in your business life?

DAY TWO – OWNERSHIP

Read Psalm 24:1. *"The earth is the Lord's, and everything in it"* (NIV).

1. What does this passage teach about the ownership of your possessions and business?

OWNERSHIP and PURPOSE

2. Prayerfully evaluate your perspective on ownership of your possessions and business. Do you consistently recognize that the Lord owns the business? Give an example of where you have or haven't recognized His ownership.

3. What can you do to more consistently acknowledge His ownership?

DAY THREE – CONTROL

Read 1 Chronicles 29:11-12. *"We adore you as being in control of everything. Riches and honor come from you alone, and you are the Ruler of all mankind; your hand controls power and might, and it is at your discretion that men are made great and given strength"* (TLB).

And read Psalm 135:6. *"Whatever the Lord pleases, He does, in heaven and in earth. . . ."*

1. What do these verses say about the Lord's control of your circumstances?

Read Isaiah 40:21-24. *"Do you not know? Have you not heard? . . . He sits enthroned above the circle of the earth, and its people are like grasshoppers. He stretches out the heavens like a canopy, and spreads them out like a tent to live in. He brings princes to naught and reduces the rulers of this world to nothing. No sooner are they planted, no sooner are they sown, no sooner do they take root in the ground, than he blows on them and they wither . . ."* (NIV).

2. What does this passage tell you about the Lord's control of people?

3. Do you currently feel that God is in control of the events in your life? If not, how can you give back control to the Lord?

OWNERSHIP and PURPOSE

13

Read Genesis 45:5, 8; 50:20. *"Do not be grieved or angry with yourselves, because you sold me [Joseph] here, for God sent me before you to preserve life. . . . It was not you who sent me here, but God. . . . As for you, you meant evil against me, but God meant it for good in order to . . . preserve many people alive."*

And read Romans 8:28. *"We know that God causes all things to work together for good to those who love God, to those who are called according to His purpose."*

4. Why is it important to realize that God controls and uses even difficult circumstances for good in the life of a godly person?

5. Share a difficult circumstance you have experienced in business and how the Lord ultimately used it for good in your life.

DAY FOUR – PROFESSIONS

1. What are the professions of some of the best-known people of faith in these passages?

Abraham *(Genesis 13:2, 7)* —

Joseph *(Genesis 41:39-44)* —

Moses *(Exodus 3:1)* —

Samuel *(1 Samuel 3:20)* —

David *(2 Samuel 5:3)* —

2. Why do you think that most of these people of faith were not religious professionals?

3. Why do you think people don't need to be full-time religious professionals (serve as pastors, missionaries, or on the staff of a ministry) before they can have a real impact for Christ? How does this perspective influence the way you view your work?

Read Ephesians 2:10. *"For we are His workmanship, created in Christ Jesus for good works, which God prepared beforehand, that we should walk in them."*

4. What do you think the Lord has created and equipped you to do for a career?

DAY FIVE – YOUR TRUE BOSS

Read Colossians 3:23-24. *"Whatever you do, do your work heartily, as for the Lord rather than for men; knowing that from the Lord you will receive the reward of the inheritance. It is the Lord Christ whom you serve."*

1. For whom do you really work? How will understanding this change your perspective on work?

2. What will you do to remind yourself that you are working for Christ?

DAY SIX – CASE STUDY AND APPLICATION

Note: You may read the Ownership and Purpose Notes prior to completing Day Six Homework if you wish.

CASE STUDY

Ted Johnson was a committed Christian who had founded his company to glorify Christ. His company was having a significant impact for Christ on many people. It was also extremely fast growing and successful.

A large corporation approached Ted with an offer to purchase his company. The offering company was reputable and, while not a direct competitor, was very influential in Ted's market niche.

Ted could see the advantages to the sale. The financial resources and reputation of the offering company would provide quicker market penetration and increased profits. More people could be employed. Also, Ted would be released from personal debt that was a source of real stress and receive a sizable amount of cash. He could give much more generously to his church and other ministries. Ted is 55 and has no one who could succeed him to lead the business.

The downside was that the ownership and ultimate decision-making control would be transferred to the purchasing company, with no guarantees that the Christian focus would be continued.

Analysis

1. Define the problem/issue.

2. List the pros and cons of the sale.

3. What are the options and potential consequences?

4. What actions do you think should be taken? Why?

5. How would God be honored and glorified by these actions?

Application

Based on this case study and what you have learned from the Ownership and Purpose lesson, answer the following questions.

1. What insight have you gained concerning your business?

2. What changes might you need to make in the operation of your business?

3. What results would you hope to see?

4. Complete the Quit Claim Deed on the following page, transferring ownership of your possessions and business to the Lord.

Quit Claim Deed

This Quit Claim Deed, Made the _____ day of _____

From: _____

To: The Lord

I (we) hereby transfer to the Lord the ownership of the following:

Witnesses who hold me (us) accountable
in the recognition of the Lord's ownership:

_____

_____

_____

_____

Stewards of the possessions above:

_____

_____

OWNERSHIP and PURPOSE NOTES

Please complete the Ownership and Purpose Homework (Days 1-5) before reading these notes.

As a young boy, Henry Crowell heard Evangelist Dwight Moody issue the challenge to be wholly committed to God's service. Henry promised God that if He would use him to make money, he would supply it to those working for the Lord. He would conduct his business for God's glory. After winning a battle with tuberculosis, Henry Crowell founded Quaker Oats. Under Crowell's leadership, the company grew and enjoyed remarkable success.

Henry Crowell had been tithing (giving 10 percent of his income) since he was a boy. However, in 1898, Henry and his wife were transformed as the result of a small-group Bible study. The group began a study on the subject of property. "Not only are we to live for Christ," he said, "everything we have belongs to God. Bank accounts, businesses, stocks, bonds, real estate—everything. We are simply stewards and managers for God of all that He has."

Henry's perception of his business dramatically changed. He considered himself promoted from the status of a person conducting his own business to that of a person entrusted with the affairs of God.

Crowell's faith was set on fire. He became an extraordinary giver and a leader in the church and community. He volunteered one day each week to work for Moody Bible Institute and is credited for doing more than any other person to build that remarkable ministry.

Henry Crowell had settled the major foundational issues for the Christian businessperson: ownership and purpose.

> *The Lord owns our possessions and businesses.*

OWNERSHIP

The Lord owns our possessions and businesses. *"To the Lord your God belong . . . the earth and everything in it"* (Deuteronomy 10:14, NIV). *"The earth is the Lord's, and all it contains"* (Psalm 24:1).

Scripture even reveals specific items God owns. Leviticus 25:23 identifies Him as the owner of all the land: *"The land must not be sold permanently, because the land is mine"* (NIV). Haggai 2:8 says that He owns precious metals: *"'The silver is Mine, and the gold is Mine,' declares the Lord of hosts."* And in Psalm 50:10-12, the Scriptures tell us: *"Every beast of the forest is Mine, the cattle on a thousand hills . . . everything that moves in the field is Mine. If I were hungry, I would not tell you; for the world is Mine, and all it contains."*

The Lord created all things, and He has never transferred the ownership of His creation to people. As we will see throughout this study, recognizing God's ownership is crucial in allowing Jesus Christ to become the Lord of our businesses. He is the owner of *every* business, large or small, public or private.

OUR OWNERSHIP OR HIS LORDSHIP

If we are going to be genuine followers of Christ, we must transfer ownership of our businesses to the Lord. *"No one of you can be My disciple who does not give up all his own possessions"* (Luke 14:33). We must give up claim to the ownership of all we have. Sometimes the Lord will test our willingness to give up the very possession that is most important to us.

The most vivid example of this in Scripture is when the Lord instructed Abraham, *"Take now your son, your only son, whom you love, Isaac . . . and offer him there as a burnt offering"* (Genesis 22:2). When Abraham obeyed, demonstrating his willingness to give up his most valuable possession, God responded, *"Do not lay a hand on the boy. . . . Now I know that you fear God, because you have not withheld from me your son, your only son"* (Genesis 22:12, NIV).

When we acknowledge God's ownership, every business decision becomes a spiritual decision. No longer do we ask, "Lord, what do You want me to do with my business?" The question is restated, "Lord, what do You want me to do with Your business?"

RECOGNIZING GOD'S OWNERSHIP

Consistently recognizing God's ownership is difficult. It is easy to believe intellectually that God owns all you have and yet live as if it were not true. Here are a number of practical suggestions to help us recognize God's ownership:

- For the next 30 days, meditate on 1 Chronicles 29:11-12 when you first awake and just before going to sleep.
- Be careful in the use of personal pronouns; consider substituting "the" or "the Lord's" for "my," "mine," and "ours."
- Ask the Lord to make you aware of His ownership and help you to be willing to relinquish ownership. Pray for this during the next 30 days.

> *When we acknowledge God's ownership, every business decision becomes a spiritual decision.*

CONTROL

Besides being the Owner, God is ultimately in control of every event that occurs upon the earth. *"We adore you as being in control of everything"* (1 Chronicles 29:11, TLB). *"Whatever the Lord pleases, He does, in heaven and in earth"* (Psalm 135:6). And in the book of Daniel, King Nebuchadnezzar stated: *"I praised the Most High; I honored and glorified Him who lives forever. . . . All the peoples of the earth are regarded as nothing. He does as He pleases with the powers of heaven and the peoples of the earth. No one can hold back His hand or say to Him: 'What have you done?'"* (Daniel 4:34-35, NIV).

The Lord is in control even of difficult events. *"I am the Lord, and there is no other, the One forming light and creating darkness, causing well-being and creating calamity; I am the Lord who does all these"* (Isaiah 45:6-7).

It is important for the people of God to realize that the heavenly Father orchestrates even seemingly devastating circumstances for ultimate good in the lives of the godly. *"We know that God causes all things to work together for good to those who love God, to those who are called according to His purpose"* (Romans 8:28). The Lord allows difficult circumstances for three reasons:

1. He accomplishes His intentions.

This is illustrated in the life of Joseph, who was sold into slavery as a teenager by his jealous brothers. Joseph responded to his brothers: *"Do not be grieved or angry with yourselves, because you sold me here, for God sent me before you to preserve life. . . . It was not you who sent me here, but God. . . . As for you, you meant evil against me, but God meant it for good in order to . . . preserve many people alive"* (Genesis 45:5-8; 50:20).

2. He develops our character.

Godly character, something that is precious in the sight of the Lord, is often developed in the midst of trying times. Romans 5:3-4 reads, *"We also rejoice in our sufferings, knowing that suffering produces perseverance; perseverance, character"* (NIV).

3. He disciplines His children.

"For those whom the Lord loves He disciplines. . . . He disciplines us for our good, that we may share His holiness. All discipline for the moment seems not to be joyful but sorrowful; yet to those who have been trained by it, afterwards it yields the peaceful fruit of righteousness" (Hebrews 12:6, 10-11).

When we are disobedient, we can expect our loving Lord to discipline us, often through difficult circumstances. His purpose is to encourage us to abandon our sin and *"share His holiness."*

OUR RESPONSIBILITY

The word in the Bible that best describes our role is "steward." A steward is a manager of someone else's possessions. The Lord has given us the authority to be stewards. *"You made him ruler over the works of your [the Lord's] hands; you put everything under his feet"* (Psalm 8:6, NIV).

Our responsibility is summed up in this verse: *"Moreover it is required of stewards that one be found faithful"* (1 Corinthians 4:2, NKJV). Before we can be faithful, we must know what we are required to do. Just as the purchaser of a complicated piece of machinery studies the manufacturer's manual to learn how to operate it, we need to examine the Creator's handbook—the Bible—to determine how He wants us to handle His businesses.

It's important to realize that God loves and cares for us deeply. He has given us these business principles because He wants the best for us. Most people discover areas in which they have not been faithful. This may have led to incorrect decisions and painful consequences. Hosea 4:6 reads, *"My people are destroyed for lack of knowledge."* Don't become discouraged.

> *Our heavenly Father orchestrates seemingly devastating circumstances for ultimate good in the lives of the godly.*

FAITHFULNESS IN LITTLE THINGS

From the Lord's perspective, it is very important for us to be faithful with small things. *"He who is faithful in a very little thing is faithful also in much; and he who is unrighteous in a very little thing is unrighteous also in much"* (Luke 16:10).

How do you know if a salesperson will do a competent job of serving a large client? Evaluate how he or she has served a small client. If we have the character to be faithful with small things, the Lord knows He can trust us with greater responsibilities. Missionary statesman Hudson Taylor said, "Small things are small things, but faithfulness with a small thing is a big thing."

CALLING

The Lord intends for each of us to fulfill a specific calling or purpose. Ephesians 2:10 reads, *"We are His workmanship, created in Christ Jesus for good works, which God prepared beforehand that we should walk in them."*

Study this passage carefully. *"We are His workmanship."* Another translation says, *"We are His handiwork"* (AMPLIFIED). Each of us has been uniquely created and given special physical, emotional, and mental characteristics and abilities.

Just as God gave you unique fingerprints, you have been created like no one else in all of human history. The passage continues, *"created in Christ Jesus for good works, which God prepared beforehand that we should walk in them"* (Ephesians 2:10). The Lord created each of us for a particular task, and He endowed us with the proper skills, aptitudes, and desires to accomplish this work.

EVERY GOD-GIVEN CALLING IS EQUALLY HONORABLE

According to Scripture, there is equal dignity in all types of work. Scripture does not elevate any profession above another; a wide variety of vocations are represented. David was a shepherd and a king. Lydia was a retailer who sold purple fabric. Daniel was a government worker. Mary was a homemaker. Paul was a tentmaker. And, finally, the Lord Jesus was a carpenter. In fact, most of the godly people in the Bible had secular jobs; relatively few were religious professionals.

FULL-TIME CHRISTIAN WORK OR A SECULAR JOB

Many feel they are not serving Christ in a significant way if they remain in business. Nothing could be further from the truth!

In his book, *God Owns My Business*, Stanley Tam writes, "Although I believe in the application of good principles in business, I place far more confidence in the conviction that I have a call from God. I am convinced that His purpose for me is in the business world. **My business is my pulpit.**"

To those who earn their living through secular pursuits, it is a great comfort to know that the "call" of holy vocation carries over to all walks of life. God strategically places His children everywhere. Many believe that only the

Most of the godly people in the Bible had secular jobs; relatively few were religious professionals.

missionary or pastor is truly spiritual, but this is not true. **Your business is your ministry.** The businessperson is in a position to influence people for Christ who would rarely consider attending a church.

R.G. LeTourneau was an innovative manufacturer of heavy construction machinery. No one did more to revolutionize the methods of the industry. In his lifetime, LeTourneau registered 316 patents, and there is not a piece of heavy construction equipment manufactured today, including land scrapers, diggers, cranes, bulldozers, and even off-shore oil drilling rigs, that did not find its conceptual origins on LeTourneau's drafting table.

In the years following World War I, LeTourneau began to tinker with earth-moving machinery. Not only were he and his wife poor, they were still in debt as they tried to pay off creditors from a failed business.

LeTourneau's sister was a missionary in China, and she challenged him to really make his life count for Christ. He thought, *Sarah is a missionary, and I'm a dirt mover. She deals with spiritual things all day, but my job is to deal with material things.* He struggled with the idea of fully dedicating his life to Christ because he thought he would have to give up moving dirt, the thing he loved to do. Finally, he prayed, "Lord, if You'll help me, I'll do anything You want me to do from this day on." LeTourneau knew that God had heard his prayer because he was overwhelmed with joy.

R.G. appeared at his pastor's front door the next morning full of questions about God's direction for his life. Rather than answering, the pastor responded, "Let's go to God and find your answers there." They spent considerable time on their knees praying. The pastor finally said, "You know, Bob, God needs business men and women as well as preachers and missionaries."

LeTourneau left the pastor's home in a daze. If God needed people in business, He could certainly find a lot better material than a dirt mover with a mountain of debts. Finally, he said to himself, *Well, if that's what God wants me to be, I'll try to be His businessman.* LeTourneau was in business with the Lord—a manager for God.

LeTourneau's company, Caterpillar, grew and became fantastically successful. Most of the profits from the sale of machinery and patent rights were donated to the work of Christ. Later, LeTourneau traveled all over the world giving his testimony about what a poor dirt farmer with a sixth-grade education could do when called to serve the Lord in business.

> *"God needs business men and women as well as preachers and missionaries."*

OUR PURPOSES IN BUSINESS

There are four primary purposes for us in business.

1. To glorify God

Business owners and managers should glorify God in their personal and business lives.

In John 17:4, Jesus said, *"I have brought you [God the Father] glory on earth by completing the work you gave me to do"* (NIV). The only way to glorify the Lord in our work is to conduct our business according to the principles found in God's Word. Our work must be done without compromising God's ways. He examines our attitude and the motivation behind what we do, not just the action itself.

The Scriptures reveal that we are actually working for Jesus Christ. *"Whatever you do, do your work heartily, as for the Lord rather than for men; knowing that from the Lord you will receive the reward of the inheritance. It is the Lord Christ whom you serve"* (Colossians 3:23-24).

If you are a manager, you are Christ's manager. If you are a corporate CEO, you lead as if Christ were the Chairman of the Board. If you are a business owner, then you are the steward of Christ's business.

Glorifying God in our businesses means dealing with employers, employees, vendors, customers, and competitors as if we were dealing with Christ. Christian business leaders try to build win-win relationships, not only because it is a good business practice, but because they sincerely care about other people. That not only glorifies God but also earns the right to introduce others to the Savior.

2. *To make a profit*

One of the purposes of a business is to make a profit. Contrary to the opinion of some, there is no biblical admonition against making a profit. Profits are the by-product of a well-run business and should be considered both normal and honorable. If a business cannot generate profits, it will fail, and its ministry to employees and customers will cease.

Every Christian in business, employer and employee alike, should work to maximize profits, but never by sacrificing other principles of a biblically based business. For instance, an employer must not maximize profits by underpaying employees or by dishonestly representing products to customers.

Unfortunately, there are many reasons why businesses fail to earn a profit. Some are unprofitable because they lack an effective accounting system. Some are disorganized. Some are unable to attract good employees. Some do not understand changes in customer needs.

Experienced businesspeople know that a slight change in the external business environment can be the difference between a profit and a loss. It may have nothing to do with a lack of sales. Rather, the profits may be eaten up or misspent. Many people are driven by pride and greed to grow businesses much faster than they should. They are not content to be profitable—they want to get rich quickly. They expand too rapidly by going deeply into debt or growing faster than they can develop the necessary leadership team.

Some businesses are not profitable because the owners choose to live beyond the means of their business. They go under because of uncontrolled expenditures or because the owner draws a salary larger than the business can afford.

The commitment to being profitable means wisely building a business with a solid financial foundation and not allowing greed and presumption to put employees, investors, vendors, customers, or creditors at undue risk. It is no sin to fail in business. However, seek to conduct your business in such a way that promotes financial stability.

Every Christian in business should work to maximize profits, but never by sacrificing other principles of a biblically based business.

3. To support the work of Christ

There is a dependent relationship between those involved in Christian ministry and Christians in business. They need each other. This is not an accidental relationship; God designed it that way. Paul wrote to the Roman church, *"Since we have gifts that differ according to the grace given to us, let each exercise them accordingly: if prophecy, according to the proportion of his faith; if service, in his serving . . . or he who gives, with liberality"* (Romans 12:6-8). Then to the Corinthian church, *"God has placed the members, each one of them, in the body, just as He desired. . . . The eye cannot say to the hand, 'I have no need of you'"* (1 Corinthians 12:18, 21).

The first part of this dependent relationship is obvious. Churches and ministries cannot exist without regular, generous giving. Fortunately, the need is not limited to their side of the equation; Christian business people have a need—the need to give. Those who are called to business need to establish financial partnerships with those who are able to put money to work effectively for the sake of Christ. Giving is one of the purposes of Christians in business; it is what God has called and gifted them to do. When business men and women understand that they are strategic in funding the work of Christ, their work takes on eternal significance.

4. To spiritually impact your sphere of influence

The Lord has given you a position of influence in the workplace in order to impact your co-workers, vendors, customers, and even your competitors. If you count the family members of everyone you impact, you may have a larger "congregation" than many churches.

The Lord has appointed you to represent Him and bring His principles, values, love, and presence to your workplace. This is a platform for evangelism, for discipleship, and for influencing those around you through serving others and then communicating His message through your words and actions.

BUILDING ON THE ROCK

What makes a solid business foundation, one that will endure the ups and downs of the changing marketplace? Jesus said, *"Everyone who hears these words of Mine, and acts upon them, may be compared to a wise man, who built his house upon the rock. And the rains descended, and the floods came, and the winds blew, and burst against that house; and yet it did not fall, for it had been founded upon the rock"* (Matthew 7:24-25). No matter how hard you labor building your business, if you are not building on the solid foundation of God's Word, sooner or later the financial rains, floods, and winds will expose the inferior foundation.

Psalm 127:1 says, *"Unless the Lord builds the house, its builders labor in vain"* (NIV). This principle is applicable to business. God's principles of business are not offered "cafeteria style." In other words, you cannot choose to implement those you like and ignore the others without suffering the consequences.

If you are faithful to conduct your business God's way, you please the Lord and place yourself in the position where He is freer to use you in the lives of others.

SUGGESTED RESOURCES

Business By The Book
by Larry Burkett
Thomas Nelson Publishers
(order from Crown at 1-800-722-1976 or Crown.org)

Loving Mondays
by John D. Beckett
Intervarsity Press

Workplace Evangelism

Living Proof (book and video series)
by Jim Peterson
CBMC
(order at 800-566-2262 or Cbmc.com)

Show and Tell
by Kent and Davidene Humphreys
Moody Press
(order from your local bookstore or Amazon.com)

For a list of ministries that serve the marketplace, visit
Crown.org/Business.

> "Unless the Lord builds the house, its builders labor in vain" *(Psalm 127:1, NIV)*.

EXECUTIVE SUMMARY – CHAPTER 2

1. God owns our possessions and businesses (1 Chronicles 29:11-12).

2. Our responsibility is to be a faithful steward (manager) of everything God entrusts to us, including our business.

3. Those in business are to use their work to influence others for Christ.

4. The four primary purposes for us in business are (1) to glorify God, (2) to make a profit, (3) to give, and (4) to influence others for Christ.

OWNERSHIP and PURPOSE NOTES

LEADERSHIP

CONTENTS

God's Leader Is a Servant

"Do nothing from selfishness or empty conceit, but with humility of mind let each of you regard one another as more important than himself."

Philippians 2:3

LEADERSHIP HOMEWORK

Homework to be completed for Chapter 3

Before attending class, complete the:
☐ Scripture to Memorize
☐ Leadership Homework

SCRIPTURE TO MEMORIZE

"Do nothing from selfishness or empty conceit, but with humility of mind let each of you regard one another as more important than himself" (Philippians 2:3).

DAY ONE – REVIEW CHAPTER 2 NOTES

Read the Ownership and Purpose Notes on pages 18-24 and answer.

1. What in the Notes was particularly helpful or challenging?

2. How will you apply what you learned to your personal and business life?

DAY TWO – LEADERSHIP

Read Mark 10:42-44. *"Jesus . . . said, 'You know that those who are regarded as rulers of the Gentiles lord it over them, and their high officials exercise authority over them. Not so with you. Instead, whoever wants to become great among you must be your servant, and whoever wants to be first must be slave of all"* (NIV).

1. What does Jesus say about leadership?

2. Give some examples of His leadership style.

3. How is this contrary to the way most business leaders operate?

4. How would others describe your leadership strengths and weaknesses?

Read Philippians 2:3-4. *"Do nothing out of selfish ambition or vain conceit, but in humility consider others better than yourselves. Each of you should look not only to your own interests, but also to the interests of others"* (NIV).

5. What does this passage communicate concerning caring for others?

6. List three examples of how you care for your staff at work.

DAY THREE – BUSINESS RELATIONSHIPS

Read Ephesians 6:5-8. *"Slaves [employees], obey your earthly masters [employers] with respect and fear, and with sincerity of heart, just as you would obey Christ. Obey them not only to win their favor when their eye is on you, but like slaves of Christ, doing the will of God from your heart. Serve whole-heartedly, as if you were serving the Lord, not men, because you know that the Lord will reward everyone for whatever good he does"* (NIV).

1. What does this passage tell us about how you should relate to your superiors? List any areas in which you need to improve.

Read Ephesians 6:9. *"And masters [employers], treat your slaves [employees] in the same way. Do not threaten them, since you know that he who is both their Master and yours is in heaven, and there is no favoritism with him"* (NIV).

2. What does this verse say about how we should relate to those under our authority?

Read Psalms 78:72. *"So he [King David] shepherded them [his subordinates] according to the integrity of his heart, and guided them with his skillful hands."*

3. What are some practical ways that you can improve as a shepherd-leader at work?

Read Proverbs 12:15. *"The way of a fool is right in his own eyes, but a wise man is he who listens to counsel."*

And read Proverbs 15:22. *"Without consultation, plans are frustrated, but with many counselors they succeed."*

1. What are some benefits of seeking counsel?

   Proverbs 12:15 —

   Proverbs 15:22 —

2. What hinders you from seeking counsel?

Read Psalm 16:7. *"I will praise the Lord, who counsels me; even at night my heart instructs me"* (NIV).

And read Psalm 32:8. *"I [the Lord] will instruct you and teach you in the way you should go; I will counsel you and watch over you"* (NIV).

3. Does the Lord actively counsel His children? How?

4. Have you ever suffered for not seeking the Lord's counsel? If so, describe what happened.

Read Psalm 119:105. *"Your word is a lamp to my feet, and a light for my path"* (NIV).

And read Hebrews 4:12. *"For the Word of God is living and active. Sharper than any double-edged sword. . . . It judges the thoughts and attitudes of the heart"* (NIV).

1. Should the Bible also serve as your counselor? Why?

2. Do you consistently read and study the Bible? If not, why?

Read Proverbs 11:14. *"Where there is no guidance, the people fall. But in abundance of counselors there is victory."*

And read Ecclesiastes 4:9-10, 12. *"Two are better than one because they have a good return for their labor. For if either of them falls, the one will lift up his companion. But woe to the one who falls when there is not another to lift him. . . . If one can overpower him who is alone, two can resist him. A cord of three strands is not quickly torn apart."*

3. What do these verses say to you?

    Proverbs 11:14 —

    Ecclesiastes 4:9-10, 12 —

4. How do you propose to apply this principle in your personal and business life?

5. In your opinion, who should be the number-one counselor of a husband? Of a wife? Why?

LEADERSHIP

Read Psalm 1:1. *"How blessed is the man who does not walk in the counsel of the wicked, nor stand in the path of sinners, nor sit in the seat of scoffers."*

6. Whom should you avoid as a counselor? Why?

DAY SIX – CASE STUDY AND PRACTICAL APPLICATION

Note: You may choose to read the Leadership Notes prior to completing this Day Six Homework.

CASE STUDY

Harvey Peterson was the CEO of a small manufacturing operation who had never taken the time to document the core values of the business. He hired a plant manager. During the interview, the applicant commented that he was not a Christian but would have no problem working in a Christian environment.

The new manager freed up Harvey's time to pursue marketing and sales planning, and as a result, sales and profits increased substantially. The manager and his wife decided to use one of his first bonus checks to make the down payment on a home.

However, the new manager was lax about safety, break time limits, and plant cleanliness. Attempts to minister to the plant staff were damaged by the manager's rude and verbally abusive manner. Some key employees quit because of it. Harvey counseled the manager, but the manager made no changes.

Harvey was in doubt. If he discharged the manager, it would financially hurt the manager's family. But continuing to have him on staff would potentially damage the company's witness to the other employees.

Analysis

1. Define the problem/issue.

2. Identify the people involved.

3. What decisions must be made and what are the potential consequences?

4. What actions do you think should be taken? Why?

5. How would God be honored and glorified by these actions?

Application

Based on this case study and what you have learned from the Leadership lesson, answer the following questions.

1. What principles will you apply to your business?

2. What changes might you need to make in the operation of your business?

3. What results would you hope to see?

PRACTICAL APPLICATION

Identify the *core values* of your business or department and describe how you are going to help everyone learn and apply them.

LEADERSHIP NOTES

Please complete the Leadership Homework (Days 1-5) before reading these notes.

Dr. John Maxwell, a leading authority in the area of leadership, states, "Everything rises and falls on leadership." Leaders establish the culture of the business.

What would Jesus do if He were in your position? How would He lead your staff? How would He manage your business? Charles M. Sheldon wrote a book entitled *In His Steps*. In the story, first published in 1894, a homeless man showed up at a pastor's study looking for help. The pastor, busy preparing his sermon, gave him no more than some sympathy. On the following Sunday, in walked the sickly man. He addressed the congregation with a simple question: When you say you follow Jesus, does that mean that you're determined to do what Jesus would do? As he spoke, he collapsed and died. On the following Sunday the pastor challenged his congregation for volunteers to make a commitment—for an entire year they would do nothing without asking, "What would Jesus do?"

As the characters in Sheldon's story began to genuinely ask this question, the impact was profound. Their lives were changed along with many others they influenced in the community. (Some people today wear WWJD bracelets—an acronym for "What Would Jesus Do?")

> *Only once did Jesus say He was leaving His disciples an example—when He washed their feet to illustrate servanthood.*

JESUS CHRIST ON LEADERSHIP

Jesus reveals a radical contrast between the world's concept of leadership and biblical leadership in Mark 10:42-44: *"Those who are recognized as rulers of the Gentiles lord it over them; and their great men exercise authority over them. But it is not [to be] so among you, but whoever wishes to become great among you shall be your servant; and whoever wishes to be first among you shall be slave of all."*

Only once did Jesus say He was leaving His disciples an example—when He washed their feet to illustrate servanthood (John 13:3-17). Jesus said this about leadership, *"Do not be called leaders; for One is your Leader, that is, Christ. But the greatest among you shall be your servant. And whoever exalts himself shall be humbled, and whoever humbles himself shall be exalted"* (Matthew 23:10-12).

All Christians who serve in leadership must demonstrate the characteristics of a servant leader: unconditional love, humility, and self-sacrifice. Servant leaders encourage others, want the best for others, and help empower others. There is no place for the proud or power-hungry. It is important to note that the person chosen to lead the children of Israel out of Egyptian captivity was referred to as "Moses, My servant," not "Moses, My leader."

The leader's attitude toward power and authority

Theologian J. I. Packer wrote that one of the problems Christians face in business is how they handle power. "All power tends to corrupt persons holding it—financial and economic power. It is difficult to manage power in such a way that one neither idolizes oneself . . . nor abuses those one hires . . . but remains a humble steward of the power one has been given, using it for the benefit of others and for the glory of God." Becoming a servant leader begins by adopting Christ's attitude toward power, position, and authority.

The leader's attitude towards others

The driving concerns among most managers are their projects, their numbers, and their own advancement, even when their attention to these things is detrimental to others. One of the most common practices is taking credit for accomplishments of those whom they supervise. Then when there are problems, the first order of business is to assign blame to others. However, leaders should serve others out of humble submission to the Lord Jesus Christ. *"Do nothing from selfishness or empty conceit, but with humility of mind let each of you regard one another as more important than himself, do not merely look after your own personal interests, but also for the interests of others"* (Philippians 2:3-4).

> Becoming a servant leader begins by adopting Christ's attitude toward power, position, and authority.

The leader models diligence and sacrificial service

We should consider ways we can sacrifice for those we are leading. *"He [Jesus] laid down His life for us; and we ought to lay down our lives for the brethren"* (1 John 3:16). Christ led a life of service and sacrifice—even to the point of death. And as a leader, no one had ever been bolder when it came to demanding sacrifice and single-minded dedication from those who wanted to follow Him—even to the point of death.

Whatever you want your followers to do, you must first do. Servant leaders who follow the model of Christ actually lead their troops into battle, not considering themselves too important to work hard and sacrifice. Of course, the tasks and responsibilities of business leaders differ from those of the people they lead. They have the task of creating a business culture in which the values and purposes of the company are not just commanded but modeled from the top.

What you do, especially in difficult situations, has a much more powerful impact than anything you say. It either reinforces or negates your testimony for Christ. When a leader demonstrates the character of Christ in the way he or she works, it helps earn the right to share the reality of Christ with others.

Communicate, Communicate, Communicate

Maintaining good communication is one of the most important and difficult functions in any organization. The Vietnam War provided some excellent illustrations of this. Part of the Communist strategy for undermining the morale of POWs was to isolate them from each other to limit their ability to communicate with each other.

The POWs knew they couldn't let their captors succeed, and they took incredible risks just to keep in contact. They devised a variety of communication methods including tap codes and secret note systems. Their persistence in finding ways to communicate effectively not only encouraged those in solitary confinement but also transmitted resistance policies and intelligence on the activities of their captors. Their communication promoted unity and helped them resist the enemy's tactics so they could return with honor at the end of the war.

The Genesis account of building the tower of Babel supports the importance of good communication. At that time, everyone spoke the same language and adopted a common goal. The Lord makes this remarkable observation, *"If as one people speaking the same language they have begun to do this, then nothing they plan to do will be impossible for them"* (Genesis 11:6, NIV).

When a group of people are committed to accomplishing a particular task and there is good communication, then *"nothing they plan to do will be impossible for them"*—as long as it is within the will of God. Since building the tower was not what the Lord wanted, He stopped construction. He disrupted their ability to communicate, which was the foundation for successful completion of the tower. *"Come, let us go down and confuse their language so they will not understand each other"* (Genesis 11:7, NIV).

It's especially important to listen to employee complaints. *"If I have despised the claim of my . . . [employees] when they filed a complaint against me, what then could I do when God arises, and when He calls me to account, what will I answer Him?"* (Job 31:13-14). A sensitive, listening ear is a tangible expression that you care about the other person. When a complaint is legitimate, the employer should take appropriate steps to solve the problem.

Most organizations don't need a Communist camp commander—such as the POWs had—to foil their communication; it just seems to happen unless everyone makes communication a high priority. Without good communication, people begin to function in isolation and are likely to make incorrect assumptions. This eventually results in problems that affect relationships and profits.

We recommend both formal and informal communication systems. Regularly scheduled reports and briefings can help staff stay current on information that is crucial for decisions. Occasional informal visits are a valuable supplement, providing a firsthand perspective. When people can share things with you without fear, information will flow more freely.

Also, consider how you can most effectively utilize technology to communicate with your leadership, staff, vendors, and customers. For example, the CEO at Crown Financial Ministries sends a weekly video e-mail to about

When a group of people are committed to accomplishing a particular task and there is good communication, then "nothing they plan to do will be impossible for them"—as long as it is within the will of God.

500 key people around the globe, helping them stay current. The leadership has access to detailed information over Crown's Intranet. And tens of thousands of customers receive weekly and monthly informative e-mails.

Maintain a clear vision for your business

Although the need for a focused vision seems obvious, it's amazing how easy it is to get off track. Consider that an aircraft flying only 10 degrees off its planned course would be 10 miles off at 60 miles but more than 1,000 miles off after flying from New York to Hawaii.

A clearly defined vision or mission statement can keep you on course and serve as a benchmark to help you evaluate all new opportunities. Knowing what the Lord has called Crown to do has enabled us to stay on course, remain focused on what we do best, and avoid getting sidetracked. We believe this is one of the key reasons we've been so effective in carrying out our mission over the past 25-plus years.

As a leader, one of your key responsibilities is to communicate the vision continually so that everyone, down to the newest person, has a clear picture of what you stand for and what you want to accomplish. Quality employees now seek employment from companies whose values match their own. By providing a vision and environment that will allow individuals to realize their personal goals and fulfill part of their own missions, you will increase your potential to attract and retain people who make significant contributions.

Know your personality

The Bible teaches that each of us is a unique design with a differing array of talents. There is no one else exactly like you. That's why it's so important for you to have a realistic appraisal of how God has made you. Exercise your leadership based on your own style and not someone else's.

The questions you need to answer are: "What is my design?" and "What talents do I bring to the organization?" By having a clear picture of who you are, you are able to lead from your strengths and minimize the negative impact of your weaknesses. A realistic appraisal can greatly improve the likelihood of your long-term success.

By having a clear picture of who you are, you are able to lead from your strengths and minimize the negative impact of your weakenesses.

Eddie is a natural entrepreneur. He's a visionary who's gifted at identifying a need and then coming up with products and services to meet that need. Creativity is definitely his strength, and he is able to understand the big picture—all the way to the end. Eddie loves adventure, he's drawn to a challenge, and he likes doing something different every day.

But like the rest of us, Eddie has limitations. He doesn't anticipate the actual amount of time and resources required for projects. Since he thinks in terms of the finished product and underestimates the required detail work, he is often impatient with those working for him.

Eddie does not enjoy the day-to-day activities of the organization. He's much better at pioneering something new rather than operating the established. Eddie needs capable managers to help make his vision a reality. Good managers are usually gifted differently from entrepreneurs, yet both are equally important to an organization.

You need to be able to answer the questions: "Who am I?" and "Does the majority of my work match my strengths?" If you don't have an accurate picture of who you are, then seek counsel from your spouse and friends. Consider taking a personality assessment.

It was out of this concern that Crown developed the *Personality I.D.®* assessment to help people understand the unique blend of traits that God has given them. An abbreviated version is available as an online complementary tool and can be accessed at Crown.org/Tools/Personality.asp. The *Team Personality I.D.™* software program can be used in the workplace to help identify traits of team members and how they interact.

Develop your people

This information age requires highly trained employees. New technologies offer opportunities for significant breakthroughs in productivity—but only if employees are trained to use them. Unfortunately, changes in technology are coming so fast that current workers face a daunting challenge. Workers without access to ongoing training are quickly losing their competitive edge in the job market. This is especially true for employees whose primary experience is in old-world technology.

A common characteristic of great companies is that they invest heavily in training. One motivation of a Christlike business leader is to develop people and make them better employees—for the company's sake as well as for their own. Regardless of how long employees stay, you want them to leave feeling that they have worked hard in a great environment and are better for having been there.

Protect your staff

Jesus contrasted the difference between a good shepherd and a hired hand who doesn't care for sheep. The hireling never goes beyond what he is required to do. Insurance benefits, workers' compensation, and workplace safety are a major concern at any place of business, and the government requires certain safety measures. If you can create a safer working environment, go beyond the legal requirements to protect those who work at your business.

Internet pornography is a growing danger. Business leaders must seek to establish clear moral boundaries at work and help protect their staff from this pervasive problem. A Fortune 100 company recently discovered that 250 of its headquarters' employees were spending considerable time viewing pornography at work. A computer audit revealed that one employee averaged 37 hours per week on porn sites while at work!

Bless your staff *and* their families by imposing and enforcing a policy that strictly prohibits Internet pornography at work.

Be a steward of profits and people

Business leaders have the tension of balancing their responsibility for profits with their responsibility to care for employees. What is best for the company sometimes seems at odds with what is best for the staff. In the long run, workers never benefit from decisions that significantly damage the com-

> One motivation of a Christlike business leader is to develop people and make them better employees—for the company's sake as well as for their own.

pany's profitability.

Decisions that require sacrifices from staff are never easy to implement, even when it is clear that they are necessary. Being a faithful steward of God's business means that you are responsible for profits and financial stability as well as employee care.

THE LEADER SEEKS COUNSEL

God encourages us to use a great resource that He knows will benefit us and our business—godly counselors. Proverbs 19:20 reads, *"Listen to advice and accept instruction, and in the end you will be wise"* (NIV). Proverbs 12:15 says, *"The way of a fool is right in his own eyes, but a wise man is he who listens to counsel."*

Seek counsel to secure insights, suggestions, and alternatives that will aid you in making a proper decision. It is not the counselor's role to make the decision; you retain that responsibility.

Two common attitudes keep us from seeking counsel. The first one is pride. Our culture perceives seeking advice as a sign of weakness. We are told, "Stand on your own two feet. You don't need anyone to help make your decisions for you!"

The second attitude that keeps us from seeking counsel is stubbornness. This attitude is characterized by the statement, "Don't confuse me with the facts. My mind is already made up!" Whether we are aware of it or not, we sometimes do not want to face the facts that another person might bring to light.

What are the sources of counsel we need to seek? Before making a business decision, particularly an important one, subject it to three sources of counsel.

God encourages us to use a great resource that He knows will benefit us and our business—godly counselors.

Scripture

First, what does God's Word say about a particular issue? The Psalmist wrote, *"Your laws are both my light and my counselors"* (Psalm 119:24, TLB). Psalm 119:98-100 reads, *"Your commands make me wiser than my enemies. . . . I have more insight than all my teachers, for I meditate upon your statutes. I have more understanding than the elders, for I obey your precepts"* (NIV).

When we think of people who are skilled in business decision making, we often think of experts or those who are older and more experienced. Yet Scripture tells us we can have more insight and wisdom by searching the Bible than those who are educated and experienced in the ways of the world. I would rather obey the truth of Scripture than risk suffering the consequences of following my own inclinations or the opinions of people.

The Bible makes this remarkable claim about itself: *"The word of God is living and active and sharper than any two edged sword . . . and . . . able to judge the thoughts and intentions of the heart"* (Hebrews 4:12). The truths in the Bible are timeless. The Bible is a living book that our Lord uses to communicate His direction to all generations.

Scripture is the very first filter through which we should put a business decision. If that clearly answers a question, we do not have to go any further because the Bible contains the Lord's written, revealed will.

If the Bible provides clear direction in a matter, we know what to do. If the Bible is not specific about an issue, we should seek the second source of counsel: godly people.

Counsel of godly people

"The godly man is a good counselor, because he is just and fair and knows right from wrong" (Psalm 37:30-31, TLB). The Christian life is not one of independence from other Christians but of interdependence upon one another. This is illustrated in Paul's discussion concerning the body of Christ in 1 Corinthians 12. Each of us is pictured as a different member of this body. Our ability to function most effectively is dependent upon the members working together. God has given each of us certain abilities and gifts, but He has not given any one person all the abilities that he or she needs to be most productive.

Spouse

If you are married, the first person you need to consult is your spouse. Women tend to be gifted with a wonderfully sensitive and intuitive nature that is usually very accurate. Men tend to focus more objectively on the facts. In God's sight, a husband and wife are one. *"The two shall become one"* (Matthew 19:5). They need each other to achieve the proper balance for optimal decisions. The Lord honors a wife's "office" or "position" as helpmate to her husband. Many times the Lord communicates most clearly to a husband through his wife.

If you are a husband, regardless of her business background, you must cultivate and seek your wife's counsel. There may be times when she doesn't feel qualified to offer an opinion. You will learn through experience where her insights and interests are the strongest. Consistently seeking your spouse's advice will enable you to avoid many mistakes.

It will preserve and strengthen your relationship

Since you and your spouse will both experience the consequences of a decision, you should strive to agree beforehand. Then, even if your choice proves to be disastrous, your relationship remains intact. There are no grounds for an "I told you so" response.

When you seek your spouse's advice, you actually are communicating, "I love you. I respect you. I value your insight." Consistently asking for advice also keeps your spouse informed of your true financial condition. This is important in the event one predeceases the other or is unable to work.

Set aside time to talk

The best way to start communicating is to set aside time regularly to discuss important business decisions. It is also wise to schedule a weekend once a year to discuss long-term goals such as business growth, retirement, or sale of a business. Input from employees or board members is valuable, but it is not the same as input from your spouse. No one knows you better than your spouse.

The Christian life is not one of independence from other Christians but of interdependence upon one another.

Working with a spouse

When you and your spouse work together in business, it is important that you begin by discussing the relationship honestly. There can be only one leader, and attempting any other arrangement will damage your relationship and frustrate your employees. Clearly defining your roles is essential. If you question whether you can comfortably work in the same office or even the same company, face the issue from the outset.

Experienced people

We should also consult people with extensive experience. If you are considering expanding into manufacturing, attempt to locate the most qualified manufacturer to counsel you.

A multitude of counselors

Proverbs 15:22 reads, *"Without consultation, plans are frustrated, but with many counselors they succeed."* And Proverbs 11:14 says, *"Where there is no guidance, the people fall, but in abundance of counselors there is victory."* Each of us has a limited range of knowledge and experience; we need the input of others who bring their own unique backgrounds to give us insight and stimulate our thinking with alternatives we would never have considered without their advice.

The best way to accomplish this is to meet regularly with a small group of businesspeople to share your lives with each other, pray for each other, and be accountable. You will experience the benefits and safety of having a group of people who know you, love you and give you objective counsel even when it hurts.

Several ministries that serve the business community have developed outstanding small group experiences. Visit **Crown.org/Business** for more details.

The counsel of the Lord

During the process of analyzing the facts, searching the Bible, and obtaining the counsel of many godly people, seek direction from the Lord. This is the most important thing you can do. In Isaiah 9:6, we are told that one of the Lord's names is *"Wonderful Counselor."*

The Psalms also identify the Lord as our counselor. *"I [the Lord] will instruct you and teach you in the way which you should go; I will counsel you with My eye upon you"* (Psalm 32:8). *"You [the Lord] guide me with your counsel"* (Psalm 73:24, NIV). *"I will bless the Lord who has counseled me"* (Psalm 16:7).

Scripture provides numerous examples of the blessings of heeding God's counsel as well as the unfortunate consequences of not seeking it. After the children of Israel began their successful campaign to capture the Promised Land, some of the natives attempted to enter into a peace treaty with Israel. These natives deceived Israel's leaders into believing they were from a distant land. Joshua 9:14-15 reads, *"So the men of Israel took some of their provisions, and did not ask for the counsel of the Lord. And Joshua made peace with them and made a covenant with them, to let them live."*

Because Israel failed to seek the Lord's counsel, the Promised Land

> "Without consultation, plans are frustrated, but with many counselors they succeed" (Proverbs 15:22).

remained populated with ungodly people, and Israel became ensnared by their false gods. The leaders simply accepted the "facts" they could see—facts that were designed to deceive. In many situations, only the Lord can reveal truth and proper direction to us. Only the Lord knows the future and the ultimate consequences of a decision.

Throughout Scripture we are admonished to wait upon the Lord. Whenever you feel hurried or pressured or you experience a sense of confusion concerning a decision, discipline yourself to go to a quiet place that will allow you to listen quietly and prayerfully for His still, small voice. The world around you screams, "Hurry!" but the Lord tells you to wait.

Avoiding the counsel of the wicked

We need to avoid one particular source of counsel. *"How blessed is the man who does not walk* in *the counsel of the wicked"* (Psalm 1:1). The word "blessed" literally means to be "happy many times over." The definition of a "wicked" person is one who lives his life without regard to God. A wicked person can be either a person who does not yet personally know the Lord or one who knows Jesus Christ as Savior but is not following Him in obedience.

In our opinion, it is permissible to seek input from those who may not know Christ for facts and technical expertise, but you are responsible to make the final decision.

The excuse often given for using secular advisors is that good Christian advisors are not available. That simply is *not* true. If God's Word requires it, God provides it. Every field contains many highly competent professionals who are also committed Christians. Be diligent to locate good Christian counselors; ask other committed Christians for referrals.

 SUGGESTED RESOURCES

Leadership

The 21 Irrefutable Laws of Leadership
by John Maxwell
Thomas Nelson Publishers

Spiritual Leadership
by J. Oswald Sanders
Moody Press

Personality Testing

Personality I.D.®
Team Personality I.D.™
Crown Financial Ministries

1. Biblical leadership is to be modeled after Jesus Christ's servant-leadership.

2. Clear communication is foundational for a successful business.

3. Learn your strengths and weaknesses as a leader.

4. Seek godly counsel when making business decisions.

LEADERSHIP NOTES

Get Out of Debt

*"Just as the rich rule the poor,
so the borrower is servant to the lender."*
Proverbs 22:7, TLB

CONTENTS

FINANCE HOMEWORK

Before attending class, complete the:
☐ Scripture to Memorize
☐ Finance Homework

 SCRIPTURE TO MEMORIZE

> *"Just as the rich rule the poor, so the borrower is servant to the lender"*
> (Proverbs 22:7, TLB).

DAY ONE – REVIEW CHAPTER 3 NOTES

Read the Leadership Notes on pages 34-42 and answer.

1. What in the Notes was particularly helpful or challenging?

2. How will you apply what you learned to your personal and business life?

DAY TWO – DEBTS

Read Romans 13:8. *"Keep out of debt and owe no man anything"* (AMPLIFIED).

And read Proverbs 22:7. *"Just as the rich rule the poor, so the borrower is servant to the lender"* (TLB).

1. Is debt encouraged in Scripture? Why?

   Romans 13:8 —

   Proverbs 22:7 —

2. How does this apply to you personally and to your business?

3. If you are in debt, do you have a strategy to eliminate it? If you have a plan, please describe it.

Read Deuteronomy 28:1-2, 12. *"If you diligently obey the Lord your God, being careful to do all His commandments which I command you today, the Lord your God will set you high above all the nations of the earth. All these blessings will come upon you and overtake you, if you obey the Lord your God. . . . And you shall lend to many nations, but you shall not borrow."*

And read Deuteronomy 28:15, 43-44. *"If you do not obey the Lord your God, to observe to do all His commandments and His statutes with which I charge you today, that all these curses will come upon you. . . . The alien who is among you shall rise above you higher and higher, but you will go down lower and lower. He shall lend to you, but you will not lend to him."*

4. According to these passages, how was debt viewed in the Old Testament?

5. What was the cause of someone getting into debt (becoming a borrower) or getting out of debt (becoming a lender)?

Read Psalm 37:21. *"The wicked borrows and does not pay back, but the righteous is gracious and gives."*

And read Proverbs 3:27-28. *"Do not withhold good from those to whom it is due, when it is in your power to do it. Do not say to your neighbor, 'Go, and come back, and tomorrow I will give it,' when you have it with you."*

1. What do these verses say about debt repayment?

　　Psalm 37:21 —

　　Proverbs 3:27-28 —

2. How will you implement this principle in your business?

Read 1 Corinthians 6:1-7. *"If any of you has a dispute with another, dare he take it before the ungodly for judgment instead of before the saints? Do you not know that the saints will judge the world? And if you are to judge the world, are you not competent to judge trivial cases? Do you not know that we will judge angels? How much more the things of this life! Therefore, if you have disputes about such matters, appoint as judges even men of little account in the church! I say this to shame you. Is it possible that there is nobody among you wise enough to judge a dispute between believers? But instead, one brother goes to law against another—and this in front of unbelievers! The very fact that you have lawsuits among you means you have been completely defeated already. Why not rather be wronged? Why not rather be cheated?"* (NIV).

3. When is it acceptable to take another believer to court? Why?

Read Matthew 18:15-17. *"If your brother sins, go and show him his fault in private; if he listens to you, you have won your brother. But if he does not listen to you, take one or two more with you, so*

FINANCE

that by the mouth of two or three witnesses every fact may be confirmed. If he refuses to listen to them, tell it to the church; and if he refuses to listen even to the church, let him be to you as a Gentile and a tax collector."

4. Describe God's procedure for Christians resolving disputes among themselves.

5. Do you have a policy on how to collect past-due receivables? If so, describe it.

DAY FOUR – GIVING

Read 1 Corinthians 13:3. *"If I give all my possessions to feed the poor . . . but do not have love, it profits me nothing."*

And read 2 Corinthians 9:7. *"Each one must do just as he has purposed in his heart, not grudgingly or under compulsion, for God loves a cheerful giver."*

1. What do these passages say about the importance of the proper attitude in giving?

   1 Corinthians 13:3 —

   2 Corinthians 9:7 —

2. How do you think you can develop the proper attitude in giving?

3. After prayerfully evaluating your attitude in giving, how would you describe it?

Read Acts 20:35. *"Remember the words of the Lord Jesus, that He Himself said, 'It is more blessed to give than to receive.'"*

4. How does this principle from God's economy differ from the way most people view giving?

Read Proverbs 11:24-25. *"There is one who scatters, and yet increases all the more, and there is one who withholds what is justly due, and yet it results only in want. The generous man will be prosperous, and he who waters will himself be watered."*

And read Luke 12:34. *"For where your treasure is, there your heart will be also."*

5. List the benefits for the giver that are found in these passages:

Proverbs 11:24-25 —

Luke 12:34 —

DAY FIVE – AMOUNT TO GIVE

Read Malachi 3:8-11. *"'Will a man rob God? Yet you are robbing Me! But you say, "How have we robbed You?" In tithes and offerings. You are cursed with a curse, for you are robbing Me, the whole nation of you! Bring the whole tithe into the storehouse, so that there may be food in My house, and test Me now in this,' says the Lord of hosts, 'if I will not open for you the windows of heaven and pour out for you a blessing until it overflows. Then I will rebuke the devourer for you, so that it will not destroy the fruits of the ground; nor will your vine in the field cast its grapes,' says the Lord of hosts."*

1. Was the tithe (giving 10 percent) required under Old Testament Law? How do you think it applies today?

Read 2 Corinthians 8:1-5. *"Brothers, we want you to know about the grace that God has given the Macedonian churches. Out of the most severe trial, their overflowing joy and their extreme poverty welled up in rich generosity. For I testify that they gave as much as they were able, and even beyond their ability. Entirely on their own, they urgently pleaded with us for the privilege of sharing in this service to the saints. And they did not do as we expected, but they gave themselves first to the Lord and then to us in keeping with God's will"* (NIV).

2. Identify principles from this passage that should influence how much you give.

3. If you are in a position to make this decision, prayerfully seek the Lord's guidance to determine how much your business should give. If you are married, ask your spouse to join you in this determination. You will not be asked to disclose the amount.

Note: You may choose to read the Finance Notes prior to completing Day Six Homework.

CASE STUDY

Sarah was a very visible Christian in the community. Her construction supply business had grown substantially for several years during prosperous times in the local economy. Credit was readily available, and Sarah had borrowed extensively, leveraged her receivables, and cosigned the notes to expand the business. She was required to provide monthly financial statements as a condition of the financing.

The economy slowed, sales were off, and there were rumors that her lender was preparing to discontinue lending to the construction industry. The current month's financial statement reflected a moderate loss, and Sarah was afraid that her credit line would be closed if she didn't continue to show a profit.

She had received a large order that was to be shipped next month. If it were included in the current financials, the company would show a profit for the month. Sarah was confident that the rest of next month's sales would be sufficient to make up the difference.

Analysis

1. Define the problem/issue.

2. Identify the people involved.

3. Identify special circumstances and potential consequences.

4. What actions do you think should be taken? Why?

5. How would God be honored and glorified by these actions?

Application

Based on this case study and what you have learned from the Finance lesson, answer the following questions.

1. What insight have you gained concerning your business?

2. What changes might you need to make in the operation of your business?

3. What results would you hope to see?

PRACTICAL APPLICATION

Complete the Debt List on the following page, and describe below your plan for reducing or eliminating your business debt.

Debt List

Date: _____

Personal Debt	Monthly Payments	Balance Due	Scheduled Pay Off Date	Interest Rate	Payments Past Due
Total Personal Debt					

Auto Loans					
Total Auto Loans					

Home Mortgages					
Total Home Mortgages					

Business Debt					
Total Business Debt					

FINANCE

FINANCE NOTES

Please complete the Finance Homework (Days 1-5) before reading these notes.

Almost every decision in business has a financial impact. Consequently, businesspeople need to understand God's principles that relate to finances, including:

- Borrowing
- Lending
- Collections
- Discounting
- Business giving

THE BIBLE ON BORROWING

Debt is *not* specifically prohibited in Scripture, but it is discouraged. It is always presented in a negative context and with warnings about its misuse. Read the first portion of Romans 13:8 from several different Bible translations: *"Owe no man any thing"* (KJV). *"Let no debt remain outstanding"* (NIV). *"Pay all your debts"* (TLB). *"Owe nothing to anyone"* (NASB). *"Keep out of debt and owe no man anything"* (AMPLIFIED).

DEBT IS CONSIDERED SLAVERY

In Proverbs 22:7, we learn why our Lord discourages debt: *"Just as the rich rule the poor, so the borrower is servant to the lender"* (TLB). When we are in debt, we are in a position of servitude to the lender. The deeper we are in debt, the more of a servant we become. We do not have the full freedom or discretion to decide where to spend our income. We have obligated ourselves legally to meet our debts.

DEBT WAS CONSIDERED A CURSE

In the Old Testament, being out of debt was one of the promised rewards for obedience. *"If you diligently obey the Lord your God, being careful to do all His commandments which I command you today, the Lord your God will set you high above all the nations of the earth. All these blessings will come upon you and overtake you, if you obey the Lord your God. . . . And you shall lend to many nations, but you shall not borrow"* (Deuteronomy 28:1-2, 12).

However, indebtedness was one of the curses inflicted for disobedience. *"If you do not obey the Lord your God, to observe to do all His commandments*

> *Indebtedness was one of the curses inflicted for disobedience.*

and His statutes with which I charge you today, that all these curses shall come upon you. . . . The alien who is among you shall rise above you higher and higher, but you will go down lower and lower. He shall lend to you, but you will not lend to him" (Deuteronomy 28:15, 43-44).

There are three fundamental biblical principles related to borrowing.

1. Avoid unnecessary borrowing.

Most people accept borrowing as a necessity and don't have a plan for their businesses to become debt free. Businesses that have debt are more vulnerable to a downturn in the economy.

Much borrowing is based on the presumption that the future is predictable. We plan for our job to continue or our business to be profitable. Scripture cautions us against presumption: *"Come now, you who say, 'Today or tomorrow, we shall go to such and such a city, and spend a year there and engage in business and make a profit.' Yet you do not know what your life will be like tomorrow"* (James 4:13–14).

2. Seek to avoid personally guaranteeing business debt.

When you personally endorse a note, you pledge all of your assets as collateral. You personally guarantee its payment. This is *personal surety*. Many people sign as surety on business debts and don't realize it. As long as the debt exists, everything you own is at risk. Proverbs 22:26-27 graphically illustrates this: *"Do not be among those who give pledges, among those who become guarantors for debts. If you have nothing with which to pay, why should he take your bed from under you?"*

When you are starting a business or your business is not financially solid, lenders will typically require you to personally guarantee its debt. But we strongly recommend that you establish the goal of eliminating the necessity of your personal guarantee for business debts.

When communicating this desire to the lender, it is essential for the lender to understand that the sole security for the debt is the business and specific assets you have pledged as collateral. The debt will be paid in cash or with the business and the assets you have pledged. But, you are not personally risking all of your assets.

Much borrowing is based on the presumption that the future is predictable. Scripture cautions us against presumption.

3. Avoid long-term debt.

"At the end of every seven years you shall grant a remission of debts" (Deuteronomy 15:1). In an era of 30-year mortgages, avoiding long-term debt sounds almost impossible. Long-term debt, however, is a relatively new idea. Our grandfathers, even many of our fathers, would have considered loans that extended for three or four decades to be unthinkable. Develop a plan to become debt free within a relatively short period of time.

PERILS OF DEBT

There are two potential dangers associated with the use of business debt.

FINANCE NOTES

1. Borrowing can hamper creativity.

Dewey Kemp and Bill Geary started an office supply business from scratch. They felt the Lord leading them to grow the new business without borrowing. This forced them to be creative. Instead of going into the retail market, they decided to serve the business community, choosing only those customers who committed to pay within 15 days of purchase. They used technology to streamline customer ordering and reduce their staffing requirements. They carried only a small inventory of frequently ordered items and their wholesale supplier made daily deliveries of other items their customers ordered. Dozens of such creative decisions allowed Dewey and Bill to build a thriving business without credit. Evaluate your business. What creative changes could you make to operate without debt?

2. Borrowing can delay necessary decisions.

Often a business that is in financial trouble because of poor management or other problems will sustain itself by borrowing instead of resolving the real problems. God's Word says, *"The prudent sees the evil and hides himself, but the naive go on, and are punished for it"* (Proverbs 22:3). The use of borrowed money can provide a false sense of security that allows a correctable situation to grow into an out-of-control problem.

Although Eastern Airlines was regularly losing money in the late '70s, the appreciating value of equipment and other assets enabled the management to borrow more and more money to sustain operations. If credit had not been available, the company would have been forced to face reality and reduce overhead or close its doors. Instead, the borrowing continued into the next decade until a speculator bought the company, cut it into pieces, and sold off the pieces. Thousands of employees lost their jobs and disrupted their families' lives. When borrowing delays the pain of necessary budget decisions, it usually results in a much greater pain.

WHEN CAN WE OWE MONEY?

Scripture is silent on the subject of when we can owe money in a business. In our opinion, it is sometimes acceptable to incur debt for a business. There are many factors that determine the appropriate limitation of debt for your business. Here are several general considerations.

1. Your personal tolerance to debt should be balanced with responsibilities to others.

Individuals vary greatly in their level of comfort with business debt and the question of how much is too much. But as a steward who is responsible for God's business, it's not only about your personal risk tolerance. If you are responsible for a family or for employees, you have to balance your risk tolerance with your responsibilities as God's steward.

2. What is at risk?

How is your debt collateralized? If you are unable to repay the debt, what are you going to lose? Will it be the new piece of equipment? Or, will it be everything you own? Attempt to collateralize all business loans *without* your personal guarantee.

3. What does your spouse think?
From a biblical perspective, you need to seek the counsel of your spouse if you are married. What does your spouse think about the debt level? Financial stress is one of the major causes of divorce; be faithful to communicate.

HOW TO GET OUT OF DEBT
Here are six steps for getting out of debt. The goal is D-Day—Debtless Day—when your business becomes absolutely free of debt.

1. Pray.
In 2 Kings 4:1-7, a widow was threatened with losing her children to her creditor, and she appealed to Elisha for help. Elisha instructed the widow to borrow many empty jars from her neighbors. The Lord supernaturally multiplied her only possession—a small quantity of oil—and all the jars were filled. She sold the oil and paid her debts to free her children.

The same God who provided supernaturally for the widow is interested in your business becoming free from debt. The first and most important step is to pray. Seek the Lord's help and guidance in your journey toward Debtless Day. He can either act immediately, as in the case of the widow, or slowly over time. In either case, prayer is essential.

A trend is emerging. As businesses begin to accelerate debt repayment, the Lord has blessed their faithfulness. Even if you can afford only a small monthly prepayment of your debt, please do it. The Lord can multiply your efforts.

Even if you can afford only a small monthly prepayment of your debt, please do it. The Lord can multiply your efforts.

2. Evaluate your financial situation.
Seek to eliminate unnecessary expenses that could be applied to debt reduction. Evaluate your business assets to determine if there is anything you do not need that might be sold to help you get out of debt more quickly. Seek the counsel of competent business people to help you analyze your financial situation and business model.

3. Establish a debt repayment schedule.
Establish a repayment schedule based on these factors:

- Pay off small debts first. You will be encouraged as they are eliminated, and this will free up cash to apply against other debts. After you pay off the first debt, apply its payment toward the next debt you wish to retire. After the second debt is paid off, apply what you were paying on the first and second debts toward the next debt you wish to eliminate, and so forth.
- Pay off higher-interest-rate debts. Determine what rate of interest you are being charged on each debt, and focus on those that charge the highest rate of interest.

4. Accumulate no new debt.

A key in your business becoming debt free is to stop borrowing additional money as soon as possible. If your business has been dependent upon growing debt, ask the Lord for His creativity, direction, and wisdom to eliminate the necessity of continued borrowing.

5. Communicate with your creditors.

If you are unable to pay on time, immediately communicate with your creditors. Explain your circumstances and provide them a realistic debt repayment schedule. It is rare for a borrower to do this, and most creditors will be appreciative.

6. Do not give up!

The last step may be the most difficult. It is hard work getting out of debt, but it is worth the struggle. And it is not impossible. Some of the largest companies, such as Microsoft and Cisco, operate without the use of debt.

BANKRUPTCY

In bankruptcy, a court of law declares that an entity (person or business) is unable to pay its debts. Depending upon the type of bankruptcy, the court may allow the debtor to develop a plan to repay his creditors, or the court will distribute the debtor's property among the creditors as payment for the debts.

An epidemic of bankruptcy is sweeping our country. Should a godly person declare bankruptcy? The answer is generally no. Psalm 37:21 tells us, *"The wicked borrows and does not pay back, but the righteous is gracious and gives."*

However, in our opinion, bankruptcy is permissible under two circumstances:

- if a creditor forces a person into bankruptcy, or
- if a counselor believes the debtor's emotional health is at stake because of inability to cope with the pressure of unreasonable creditors.

After bankruptcy, seek counsel from a competent attorney to determine how it is legally permissible to attempt to repay the debt. Make every effort to repay the debt. For a large debt, this may be a long-term goal that is largely dependent on the Lord's supernatural provision of resources.

Priority of repayment: We recommend that the repayment priority should be in the same order in which goods or services were received.

THE BIBLE ON LENDING

Unless you are paid in full every time you sell your products, you are in the lending business. In particular, wholesalers, contractors, distributors, and professional services usually have to deal with credit in the form of their accounts receivable.

Should Christians be in the credit business? There is nothing biblically wrong with extending credit to qualified customers. As we have already learned, God promised Old Testament believers that they would be blessed if they obeyed His commandments. One of those blessings had to do with lending. *"The Lord will . . . bless all the work of your hand; and you shall lend to many nations, but you shall not borrow"* (Deuteronomy 28:12).

Just because lending is a part of "the blessing" doesn't mean we can simply forge ahead without considering how to extend credit in a way that is both honoring to God and consistent with biblical principles. You must answer the questions: To whom do we extend credit, how much credit, and what do we do about collections and accounts receivable?

TO WHOM AND HOW MUCH CREDIT DO YOU EXTEND?

Many businesses fail because of poor credit policies. Business leaders must be wise in their approach to lending. Business-to-business credit extended by wholesalers and distributors is often used as a means of managing cash flow. Customers who place orders even when they have outstanding balances extending beyond 60, 90, or 120 days are probably using your credit to fund other aspects of their business. Be careful that you are not too eager to extend credit in order to make a sale. In doing so, you may inadvertently become the financial backer of failing businesses.

Doing business by biblical principles requires that we manage our credit in such a way that we keep bad debts at a minimum. Most companies sue others or turn them over to collection without giving it a second thought. For them, it is simply a part of doing business. We are not to operate like that. We are to conduct business by a higher standard. Remember, our purpose in business is to glorify God and to sincerely care about customers even if we don't know them personally.

> *Our purpose in business is to glorify God and to sincerely care about customers even if we don't know them personally.*

SHOULD DEBTORS HAVE TO PAY?

That sounds like a silly question, but if you've been in business for a while, you know that some debtors feel no sense of obligation to pay their bills. However, from a biblical perspective there is no option when it comes to repaying. Psalm 37:21 says, *"The wicked borrows and does not pay back, but the righteous is gracious and gives."*

There is one thing you should keep in mind when it comes to lending. How many times have you heard someone say, "I can't pay you because I haven't been paid by those who owe me!" You are committed to pay your creditors whether or not your debtors pay you. That should make you think carefully about how much credit you extend and to whom.

LENDING SUMMARY

Follow these two simple principles:

- Limit your lending to those who are faithful in repaying.
- Do not extend credit to those who will be damaged by it.

What happens when people don't pay? You will discover that if you live by God's principles, your ability to collect a delinquent debt is limited because many common means of collection are unscriptural. It is important, therefore, that you determine how much you can afford to lose before extending credit to others.

Since collecting bad debts can be such an unpleasant part of business, some owners don't want to know what their employees or collection agencies are doing to handle it. The solution is not that simple, however; owners and CEOs are responsible for everything that goes on in the company. You cannot divorce yourself from what others do on your behalf. Any individual or agency that represents your business makes an impact on your reputation and your witness to the world. It is your responsibility to ensure that your agents (attorneys, collectors, and negotiators) represent not only your financial interests but your values as well.

LITIGATION WITH OTHER CHRISTIANS

Tens of thousands of lawsuits are filed each day in the United States. Unfortunately, many of these suits pit Christian against Christian.

Many factors contribute to this flood of lawsuits, including an avalanche of new laws and, most disturbingly, people becoming less and less forgiving. The court system uses an adversarial judicial process that frequently creates animosities and fractures relationships between parties. Instead of trying to heal the wounds, the system provides a legal solution but leaves the problems of unforgiveness and anger untouched.

ANALYZE YOUR MOTIVES

If you sincerely believe that everything you have belongs to God and that you are just a manager for Him, then you must make every decision with that in mind. If the motive behind your system of collections is greed, anger, or resentment, then it is *your* money you're collecting, not God's. You have a right to the money that is owed you, but if you are willing to violate the principles God has established for recovering that money, your loss is much more than a financial one.

THE PROCESS

The Bible stresses that the goal should be reconciliation. *"If therefore you are presenting your offering at the altar, and there remember that your brother has something against you, leave your offering there before the altar, and go your way; first be reconciled to your brother"* (Matthew 5:23-24).

Scripture states that when Christians are at odds with each other, they should try not to settle their disputes through the courts.

"Does any one of you, when he has a case against his neighbor, dare to go to law before the unrighteous, and not before the saints? Or do you not know that the saints will judge the world? And if the world is judged by you, are you not competent to constitute the smallest law courts? Do you not know that we shall

It is your responsibility to ensure that your agents represent not only your financial interests but your values as well.

judge angels? How much more, matters of this life? If then you have law courts dealing with matters of this life, do you appoint them as judges who are of no account in the church? I say this to your shame. Is it so, that there is not among you one wise man who will be able to decide between his brethren, but brother goes to law with brother, and that before unbelievers? Actually, then, it is already a defeat for you, that you have lawsuits with one another. Why not rather be wronged? Why not rather be defrauded?" (1 Corinthians 6:1-7).

Instead of initiating a lawsuit, a three-step procedure for Christians to resolve their differences is set forth in Matthew 18:15-17: *"If your brother sins, go and show him his fault in private; if he listens to you, you have won your brother. But if he does not listen to you, take one or two more with you, so that by the mouth of two or three witnesses every fact may be confirmed. If he refuses to listen to them, tell it to the church; and if he refuses to listen even to the church, let him be to you as a Gentile and a tax collector."*

So with that in mind, how should Christians approach collecting a debt from another Christian? That process could be expressed in modern culture this way.

- **Go in private.** Contact the debtor yourself (or in the case of a large company, through your representative) to work out a payment plan. There may be extenuating circumstances that limit your debtor's ability to pay. Offer them a chance to discuss their difficulties.
- **Go with one or two others.** If that fails, try to get them to meet with a Christian debt counselor to work out an arrangement.
- **Go before the church.** If your debtor doesn't seem to be willing to work with you, see if he or she would be willing to submit to Christian arbitration. If the debtor is unwilling to try to resolve the matter, you have the option of a collection agency or the courts. In the case of a collection agency, we recommend selecting one that practices similar values as your business.

The greatest benefit of following this procedure is not simply reaching a fair settlement of the dispute, but practicing forgiveness and demonstrating love.

COLLECTING FROM THOSE WHO DO NOT KNOW CHRIST

We recommend that a similar process of collecting past-due bills be used with those who do not know Christ. In a one-on-one contact in which you show respect for the person, attempt to work out a payment plan. If this fails, encourage the person to meet with a debt or business counselor. If that also fails, you have the option of a collection agency or the courts.

Make every decision in light of your primary function—to glorify God. If you are a business owner, carefully consider the following verse before you make a decision to sue anyone over a *personal* loss. *"Give to everyone who asks of you, and whoever takes away what is yours, do not demand it back"* (Luke 6:30).

COLLECTING FOR A PUBLIC COMPANY

When you work for a public company, you have the legal fiduciary responsibility to act for the benefit of the stockholders. You may not have as much freedom to forgive debts. However, you can still model the love of Christ by your respectful and reasonable communication with those who are past due.

THE BIBLE ON GIVING

The principle of giving from a business is not much different than giving from personal income. Actually, most of the Old Testament Scriptures on giving deal with business-generated income since few people were actually employees in the sense they are today. The majority of people in Old Testament times were self-employed in agriculture.

One of the purposes of being in business is to fund the work of God, which includes the local church, ministries, and support for those in need. The profitability of your business determines the extent to which it *can* give. Your own sense of vision and purpose determines the level at which it *will* give.

GIVING WITH AN ATTITUDE

God evaluates our giving on the basis of our attitude. *His* attitude in giving is best summed up in John 3:16: *"For God so loved the world, that He gave His only begotten Son."* Note the sequence. Because God loved, He gave. He set the example of giving motivated by love.

An attitude of love in giving is crucial: *"If I give all my possessions to feed the poor . . . but do not have love, it profits me nothing"* (1 Corinthians 13:3). It is hard to imagine anything more commendable than giving everything to the poor. But if it is done with the wrong attitude, without love, it does not benefit the giver whatsoever.

Our basis for giving out of a heart filled with love is the recognition that our gifts, though given for the benefit of people, are actually given to the Lord Himself. An example of this is Numbers 18:24: *"The tithe of the sons of Israel, which they offer as an offering to the Lord, I have given to the Levites for an inheritance."* If giving is merely to a church, a ministry, or a needy person, it is only charity. But if it is to the Lord, it becomes an act of worship. Because God is our Creator, our Savior and our Faithful Provider, we can express our love by giving our gifts to Him.

We also are to give cheerfully. *"Let each one do just as he has purposed in his heart; not grudgingly or under compulsion; for God loves a cheerful giver"* (2 Corinthians 9:7). The original Greek word for "cheerful" is *Hilarios*, which translates as the English word "hilarious." We are to be hilarious givers!

How do we develop this hilarity in our giving? Consider the early churches of Macedonia. *"Now, brethren, we wish to make known to you the grace of God which has been given in the churches of Macedonia, that in a great ordeal of affliction their abundance of joy and their deep poverty overflowed in the wealth of their liberality"* (2 Corinthians 8:1-2).

How did the Macedonians, who were in terrible circumstances—*"their great affliction and deep poverty"*—still manage to give with an *"abundance of joy"*? The answer is in verse 5: *"They first gave themselves to the Lord and to us by the will of God."* The key to cheerful giving is to submit ourselves to Christ, asking Him to direct how much He wants us to give. Only then are we in a position to give with the proper attitude and reap any of the advantages.

Stop and examine yourself. What is your attitude toward giving?

BENEFITS OF GIVING

Obviously, a gift benefits the recipient. The local church continues its ministry, the hungry are fed, and missionaries are sent. But in God's economy, the giver benefits more than the receiver. *"Remember the words of the Lord Jesus, that He Himself said, 'It is more blessed to give than to receive'"* (Acts 20:35). As we examine Scripture, we find that the giver benefits in four areas:

- **Increase in intimacy.** Above all else, giving directs our attention and heart to Christ. Matthew 6:21 tells us, *"For where your treasure is, there your heart will be also."* This is why it is so necessary to give each gift to the person of Jesus Christ. When you give your gift to Him, your heart will automatically be drawn to the Lord.

- **Increase in heaven.** Matthew 6:20 reads, *"But lay up for yourselves treasures in heaven, where neither moth nor rust destroys, and where thieves do not break in and steal."* The Lord tells us that there really is something akin to the "First National Bank of Heaven." And He wants us to know that we can invest for eternity.

  Paul wrote, *"Not that I seek the gift itself, but I seek for the profit which increases to your account"* (Philippians 4:17). There is a literal account for each of us in heaven that we will be privileged to enjoy for eternity. And while it is true that we "can't take it with us," Scripture teaches that we can make deposits to our heavenly account before we die.

- **Increase on earth.** Many people believe that giving results in only spiritual blessings, not material ones, flowing to the giver. Some who hold this view are reacting to those who teach what I call "giving to get." However, Proverbs 11:24-25 reads, *"There is one who scatters, yet increases all the more, and there is one who withholds what is justly due, and yet it results only in want. The generous man will be prosperous, and he who waters will himself be watered."* The Lord produces a material increase so that we may give even more.

  When we give, we should do so with a sense of expectancy—anticipating that the Lord will provide a material increase. What we never know is when or how the Lord may choose to provide this increase, and He can be very creative! Remember, the giver can reap the advantages of giving only when he gives cheerfully out of a heart filled with love. This clearly precludes the motive of giving just to get.

"But lay up for yourselves treasures in heaven, where neither moth nor rust destroys, and where thieves do not break in and steal" (Matthew 6:20).

63

- **Enrichment of the company's culture.** A significant benefit of business giving is the development of a culture of generosity within the business. Jess Carter owns a bank holding company that gives 10 percent of its net profit. His leadership team helps decide where the money is given, and the bank staff members are encouraged to submit giving opportunities. This has served to create an environment of generosity in which the entire staff has increased their personal giving.

AMOUNT TO GIVE

Let's survey what the Scripture says about how much to give. Prior to Old Testament Law, we find two instances of giving with a known amount. In Genesis 14:20, Abraham gave 10 percent, a tithe, of the spoils to Melchizedek after the rescue of his nephew Lot. In Genesis 28:22, Jacob promised to give the Lord a tenth of all his possessions if God brought him safely through his journey.

The Law required a tithe. The Lord condemns the children of Israel in Malachi 3:8-9 for not tithing properly: *"Will a man rob God? Yet you are robbing Me! But you say, 'How have we robbed You?' In tithes and offerings. You are cursed with a curse, for you are robbing Me, the whole nation of you!"* In addition to the tithe, the Law specified various offerings.

In the New Testament, the tithe is neither specifically required nor rejected. The instruction is to give in proportion to the material blessing we have received—with special commendation for sacrificial giving.

What we like about the tithe is that it is systematic, and the amount of the gift is easy to compute. The danger of the tithe is that it can be treated as simply another bill to be paid. If we do not have the correct attitude regarding the tithe, we do not put ourselves in a position to receive the blessings God has for us in giving. Another potential danger of tithing is the view that once we have tithed, we have fulfilled all our obligations to give. For many of us, the tithe should be the beginning of our giving, not the limit of our giving.

So, how much should you give? To answer this question, first give yourself to the Lord. Submit yourself to Him. Earnestly seek His will for you in this area, asking Him to help you obey Christ's leading. We are convinced that we should tithe from our businesses as a minimum and then give over and above the tithe as the Lord prospers and directs us.

SHOULD MY BUSINESS GIVE/TITHE FROM NET OR GROSS INCOME?

The Bible says, *"Honor the Lord from your wealth and from the first of all your produce"* (Proverbs 3:9). The first from all your produce can also be accurately restated as "your harvest." When a farmer brings in a crop, he has expenses associated with it. These include the wages of his laborers and his payments to suppliers and creditors.

In our opinion, most businesses should seek to give a tithe of their net income after expenses because some businesses operate on a very small margin. Grocery stores, for example, usually have a net profit of about three percent

When we give, we should do so with a sense of expectancy— anticipating that the Lord will provide a material increase.

of sales. One way to increase your profit margin is to keep your business debt-free. This will enable you to give more to the Lord's work.

One of the most generous people in business was R.G. LeTourneau, founder of Caterpillar. He said in his book, *Movers of Men and Mountains*, "I shovel the money out, and God shovels it back in—and God has a larger shovel than I do."

HOW CAN I GIVE NONCASH ASSETS?

Many godly business owners give their products or donate their services as well as money. When Crown was refurbishing its offices, for example, the owner of a window-blind company graciously donated the blinds. Real estate is another example of a noncash gift.

Company stock can be a particularly effective way to give under current tax laws. Since the tax code allows the value of a noncash gift to be claimed at its fair market value, the donor can receive a tax deduction above the actual cost.

Others have given a partial ownership in the business. That way, as the business prospers, so does the Lord's portion. This is exactly what Stanley Tamm did with his business. He gave a portion of his company stock to a foundation established to do the Lord's work. When dividends were declared, the foundation got its share. If the company is ever sold, the foundation will get its equitable portion.

THE GIFT OF GIVING

God has given many business people the gift of giving. Romans 12:6-8 reads, *"Since we have gifts that differ according to the grace given to us, each of us is to exercise them accordingly: if prophecy, according to the proportion of his faith; if service, in his serving . . . he who gives, with liberality."*

The Lord often gives people who have the ability to generate business income the desire to be generous. This gift of giving is not limited to those who give a lot. In fact, many who can give large amounts today started by giving smaller amounts from a smaller business that grew as they were faithful.

People with the gift of giving share freely, generously, and cheerfully. Carefully assess your life. Has God entrusted you with the gift of giving?

SUGGESTED RESOURCES

What the Bible Teaches About Money

> *Your Money Counts*
> by Howard Dayton
> Tyndale House Publishers
> (also available as a book on tape)

What the Bible Teaches About Giving

> *The Treasure Principle*
> by Randy Alcorn
> Multnomah Publishers
>
> *Debt-Free Living*
> by Larry Burkett
> Moody Publishing

(Note: These resources may be ordered through Crown at 1-800-722-1976 or Crown.org.)

EXECUTIVE SUMMARY – CHAPTER 4

1. Scripture discourages the use of debt, so be cautious when considering business debt.

2. Establish a goal and develop a plan to pay off your business debt.

3. Limit extending credit to those who are faithful in repaying on time.

4. Seek to collect delinquent debts in a way that respects the debtor and honors the Lord.

5. Consider giving at least 10 percent of your net income to the work of Christ.

FINANCE NOTES

HUMAN RESOURCES

CONTENTS

*"He who is faithful in a very little thing
is faithful also in much."*
Luke 16:10

Before attending class complete the:
☐ Scripture to Memorize
☐ Human Resources Homework

 SCRIPTURE TO MEMORIZE

"He who is faithful in a very little thing is faithful also in much" (Luke 16:10).

DAY ONE – REVIEW CHAPTER 4

Read the Finance Notes on pages 54-65 and answer.

1. What in the Notes was particularly helpful or challenging?

2. How will you apply what you learned to your personal and business life?

Note: Even if you don't have employees in your business, the principles you will learn in this chapter are applicable to other areas (e.g., church, professional associations) in which you serve in a leadership role.

DAY TWO – HIRING

Read Luke 6:12-13. *"Jesus went out to a mountainside to pray, and spent the night praying to God. When morning came, he called his disciples to him and chose twelve of them, whom he also designated apostles"* (NIV).

1. How much time did Jesus Christ invest praying about the selection of the 12 apostles?

2. How does this apply to you when you are seeking to hire employees? Do you consistently commit to pray?

3. Discuss the process you use when hiring.

4. Do you think you need to improve any areas of hiring? If so, what?

5. Do you hire only Christians in your business? Why or why not?

DAY THREE – PROMOTION

Read Genesis 39:5. *"It came about that from the time he [Joseph's Egyptian boss] made him overseer in his house and over all that he owned, the Lord blessed the Egyptian's house on account of Joseph."*

And read Matthew 25:23. *"His master replied, 'Well done, good and faithful servant! You have been faithful with a few things; I will put you in charge of many things. Come and share your master's happiness!'"* (NIV).

1. What are some of the things we should look for when considering a person for promotion?

   Genesis 39:5 —

   Matthew 25:23 —

Read 1 Timothy 3:2-3. *"Now the overseer must be above reproach, the husband of but one wife, temperate, self-controlled, respectable, hospitable, able to teach, not given to drunkenness, not violent but gentle, not quarrelsome, not a lover of money"* (NIV).

2. What character qualities from this passage do you look for when promoting people to leadership positions?

3. What are the most valuable insights you have learned from experience about promoting people?

4. Describe any lessons you have learned the hard way from unsuccessful promotions.

DAY FOUR — ACCOUNTABILITY

Read Matthew 25:19. *"Now after a long time the master of those slaves came and settled accounts with them."*

1. According to this passage, do you think the Lord approves of holding people accountable to be faithful in the handling of responsibilities?

2. How do you apply the principle of accountability to your staff?

Read Hebrews 12:10-11. *"He [the Lord] disciplines us for our good, so that we may share His holiness. All discipline for the moment seems not to be joyful, but sorrowful; yet to those who have been trained by it, afterwards it yields the peaceful fruit of righteousness."*

3. What does this passage say about discipline?

Read 1 Corinthians 15:33. *"Do not be deceived: 'Bad company corrupts good morals.'"*

4. According to this verse, how will a dishonest or rebellious employee influence other employees?

5. Describe the process you use to dismiss an employee.

Read Malachi 3:5. *"Then I [the Lord] will draw near to you for judgment; and I will be a swift witness . . . against those who oppress the wage earner in his wages."*

And read James 5:4. *"The pay of the laborers who mowed your fields, and which has been withheld by you, cries out against you."*

1. What do these verses say to you about paying employees fairly?

2. Do you feel you pay adequate wages? Why or why not?

Read Colossians 4:1. *"Masters [employers], grant to your slaves [employees] justice and fairness, knowing that you too have a Master in heaven."*

3. How can an employer apply this principle?

Read 1 Corinthians 12:24-26. *"God has combined the members of the body and has given greater honor to the parts that lacked it, so that there should be no division in the body, but that its parts should have equal concern for each other. If one part suffers, every part suffers with it; if one part is honored, every part rejoices with it"* (NIV).

4. How can you apply the principles of honor and recognition within the Body of Christ to a business environment?

5. What are some of the practical approaches you have used to honor faithful employees?

Note: You may choose to read the Human Resources Notes prior to completing Day Six Homework.

CASE STUDY

Chuck has been striving to make his company a platform for ministry. When it came time to replace the controller, he looked for a Christian. He found and hired a highly qualified one.

When his accounting clerk learned of the new controller, she demanded a 50 percent raise and a major promotion. She had been with the company for 11 years but was not qualified for the position she wanted. She was informed that it would not be possible to meet her demands. She resigned without notice rather than orient her new boss to the computerized accounting and payroll systems.

Five months later, Chuck was notified that the woman had filed an EEOC complaint against his company. She charged religious and gender discrimination because she had not been promoted to fill the controller's position.

Chuck had not considered the woman a candidate because she did not have the necessary professional qualifications. He obtained the best Christian labor attorney in the city to prepare his defense. After months of discussion, depositions, and briefs, the attorney assured Chuck that they had a solid case.

However, the attorney also told Chuck that the hearing process was unpredictable, and that an adverse ruling would be expensive. In the highly politicized climate in their state, anything could happen. He suggested that Chuck begin praying about the possibility of an out-of-court settlement. Should Chuck settle and put a limit on his liability or should he continue to defend himself to the end?

Analysis

1. Define the problem/issue.

2. Identify the people involved.

3. Identify special circumstances and potential consequences.

4. What actions do you think should be taken? Why?

5. How would God be honored and glorified by these actions?

Application
Based on this case study and what you have learned from the Human Resources lesson, answer the following questions.

1. What insight have you gained concerning your business?

2. What changes might you need to make in the operation of your business?

3. What results would you hope to see?

PRACTICAL APPLICATION
Describe your hiring process and policies. What changes do you feel are necessary and how will you implement them?

HUMAN RESOURCES NOTES

H uman resources, the people, are a company's most valuable asset. Companies usually work hard recruiting, training, and retaining productive workers. God places a high value on each individual, and so should we.

Note: Even if you don't have employees in your business, the principles you will learn in this chapter are applicable to other areas (e.g., church, professional associations) in which you serve in a leadership role.

HIRING DECISIONS

"You know, it seems like I never make the right hiring decisions," Stan said. "I get people who become dissatisfied, and they end up leaving within a year. What's my problem?"

"Let me ask you a question," Brandon, a business consultant, replied. "What are your criteria for hiring people?"

"I advertise in the local paper and choose from the people who apply," Stan answered.

"I don't mean how you find them," said Brandon. "I mean, what are the criteria by which you decide whom you will hire out of those who apply?"

Stan then began to describe a typical system of hiring. "I know what kind of experience is necessary to perform our tasks. We try to find people with at least two years' experience in a related industry who can live with our hourly rate of pay."

"What about work history, personal references, skill evaluation, and personality type?" Brandon asked.

"We try to check with an applicant's present or previous employers, but we don't do much beyond that. Most of those things cost too much, anyway," Stan said defensively. "Only big companies can afford to do them."

"Not so," Brandon replied. "The large companies do these things because they have found it considerably cheaper to hire the right people than to replace the wrong ones."

STEPS FOR ESTABLISHING A HIRING POLICY

1. Define jobs clearly.

In order to hire the right people, it is necessary that jobs be well defined. Often, just by reading a job description, prospective employees will see they are not qualified and eliminate themselves.

In order to hire the right people, it is necessary that jobs be well defined.

James interviewed for a position as a telephone marketer. He was intelligent, well-mannered, and articulate—all necessary qualifications for the position. He was also enthusiastic about coming to work for the company.

When James was given the written job description—answering questions over the telephone from customers—disillusionment was evident on his face. The department supervisor, Connie, asked, "Do you think you could do that job all day long?"

"Well, I think so," James replied. "But how long would I have to do this before I would have the chance to do something more interesting? I really want to meet the customers face to face," he said with enthusiasm.

Connie said later, "We need a telephone marketer. We don't need to invest several thousands of dollars in training James, who is likely to leave after a short while. He was looking for a foot in the door rather than the job we had to offer."

2. Hire the best person for the job.

This may sound self-evident, but most small businesses seldom hire the best person. Instead, they hire someone who is available.

Invest sufficient time to check references, use a personality-assessment tool, and evaluate the skills of a potential employee. Be sure to confirm integrity and ability to get along with other people. One progressive organization has their best administrative assistants participate in the interviewing process for potential administrative assistants. They know the necessary skills and the proper attitude they want from their peers. They ask penetrating questions, and over the past several years the entire administrative-assistant team has dramatically improved.

Do not accept a good candidate; search for the best. Follow the principle taught in Proverbs: *"Do you see a man skilled in his work? He will stand before kings; he will not stand before obscure men"* (Proverbs 22:29).

One suggestion: Do not hire people that you will have to motivate to work hard. Hire those who are *already* motivated to work hard. The availability of hard workers is why some of the largest manufacturers locate their new plants near farming communities. They hire hard-working farmers who simply need training to perform a new job.

3. Match the person to the job.

We are convinced that personality tests can be enormously helpful in placing the right person in the right job.

That conviction led Crown to develop the *Career Direct®* assessment program. Tens of thousands of individuals have used this program. Then Crown went a step further and developed specialized assessment programs to help companies identify the strengths of potential employees.

More complex and more expensive evaluations are available, but Crown's is very accurate and affordable. Here is how we use it with all potential employees in our organization. First, we detail the job requirements for the position we want to fill. For example, a receptionist would answer incoming calls and either route them to the appropriate departments or take messages.

One suggestion: Do not hire people that you will have to motivate to work hard. Hire those who are already motivated to work hard.

To find what combination of personality traits will make the best receptionist, we develop a benchmark for the position. We identify people who have been successful in the position and examine commonalities in their personality profiles. If it is a new position, we might solicit a profile from another company, consult a human-resources expert, or develop our own benchmark estimate by listing traits we think the position requires. Then we use the benchmark profile as a guide for hiring the receptionist we need. Research and experience will enable you to compile a profile for virtually any position.

4. Think through crucial issues ahead of time.

Hiring qualified people is easier when you develop a logical framework that can become the basis of your hiring policy. Some issues will be influenced by federal guidelines, others by your core values. Carefully think through the issues before you are under the stress of filling a critical role. One such issue is whether to hire non-Christians.

Should you hire only Christians? Many assume that by hiring only Christians they can avoid the problems that plague normal businesses. Such a notion is naïve. Professing Christians may not be truly committed to Christ; or they may not share your values. Some Christian employees exhibit many of the same work problems as non-Christians.

We believe that hiring only Christians stifles one of the greatest ministry opportunities—evangelism of employees. The biblical principle of not being unequally yoked (2 Corinthians 6:14) has sometimes been used to justify the exclusion of non-Christian employees. However, no yoke relationship exists between an employee and employer.

5. Establish a trial period.

We encourage a 90-day trial period for new employees. During this time, they can be evaluated for job performance and compatibility. Even the best hiring practices in the world will not eliminate all hiring errors. When the fit is not right, it is better for both the company and the employee to make the correction quickly.

6. Examine the character of potential managers and executive team members.

When hiring new managers who will represent you both inside the company and out, compare their character with the standards for leadership in the church.

"An overseer, then, must be above reproach, the husband of one wife, temperate, prudent, respectable, hospitable, able to teach, not addicted to wine or pugnacious, but gentle, peaceable, free from the love of money" (1 Timothy 3:2-3).

When you look for managers, look for those who can communicate the purpose and exemplify the values of your company. You also should look for character flaws that will emerge in difficult times.

When looking for executive team members, we recommend filling those key leadership positions with Christians who share your values. Executive

When hiring new managers who will represent you both inside the company and out, compare their character with the standards for leadership in the church.

team members largely establish the culture within a business and, in our opinion, this is best accomplished by committed believers.

7. *Consider meeting the spouse.*

There are factors other than personality and skill level that should be considered when hiring. For instance, if the candidate is married, it is important to verify that the spouse is also in favor of the employment opportunity. A spouse who is discontented with the job often leads to an unhappy employee.

HIRING SUMMARY

Hiring is one of the biggest challenges in business. A hire that is not successful can be discouraging for both the individual and the organization. It is also very expensive to hire the wrong person. Recruiting, training, and an unproductive employee all cost money. That is why it is so important to invest sufficient time to be sure you know what type of person you really need for the position and then gain as much information as possible before offering someone a job.

Don't forget the importance of prayer in your selection process. Spend time in prayer with your key staff. Ask God to bring the right people and help you match them to the right jobs.

Ultimately, a well-thought-out hiring process will save you headaches and money and will enable you to have the teammates you need to achieve your vision.

PROMOTION

Your business can succeed or fail based upon whom you promote. When considering a promotion, evaluate the following:

1. *Pray for the Lord's direction.*

If prayer could have been unnecessary for anyone, surely it would have been unnecessary for Jesus Christ, the sinless Son of God. However, it was one of the dominant habits of His life and a frequent theme in His teaching.

Jesus spent the night in prayer before appointing the 12 apostles. *"He went off to the mountain to pray, and He spent the whole night in prayer to His Father. And when day came, He . . . chose twelve of them, whom He also named as apostles"* (Luke 6:12-13).

Missionary statesman Hudson Taylor, said, "It is possible to move men, through God, by prayer alone." John Wesley, founder of the Methodist church, observed, "God does nothing but in answer to prayer."

Any time godly business leaders have to make promotion decisions, they should invest time asking the Lord to make His direction known.

2. *How has this person performed in the past?*

Utilize the principle found in Matthew 25:21, *"His master replied, 'Well done, good and faithful servant! You have been faithful with a few things; I will put you in charge of many things'"* (NIV).

When contemplating whom to promote, the first thing to look for is faithfulness in the present job. Have they been faithful in a few things? That might seem obvious, but it doesn't always happen that way.

"You will know them by their fruits" (Matthew 7:20). Promotion rarely changes performance. Given more responsibility, a more impressive title, or a higher salary, an employee will be no more motivated to follow through on assignments. Though there might be a temporary improvement, after the newness has worn off, true character re-emerges. Jesus said, *"He who is faithful in a very little thing is faithful also in much; and he who is unrighteous in a very little thing is unrighteous also in much"* (Luke 16:10). Increased responsibility and position only magnify one's character or lack of it.

3. Whose work is the Lord blessing?

Look for people upon whom the blessing of God rests. *"The Lord blessed the Egyptian's house on account of Joseph; thus the Lord's blessing was upon all that he owned, in the house and in the field"* (Genesis 39:5). Joseph was a slave in Egypt, and the Lord prospered his master's whole house because of His favor on Joseph.

God's favor on a person is the result of two factors: first, a person's character—integrity, faithfulness, and hard work. That is primarily the individual's responsibility. The second factor is the Lord's gift of certain skills and abilities, and His choosing to bless the person's efforts to use them. Psalm 75:6-7 reads, *"Promotion and power come from nowhere on earth, but only from God"* (TLB).

4. Do not promote people beyond their ability.

How many times have you heard of the best salesperson being promoted to the position of sales manager? And then failing miserably! The talents that made a person very productive in one role may not be the skills necessary for a position of greater responsibility. Paul understood that each of us has areas in which God has designed us to perform well, and each of us has limitations. *"Confine our boasting to the field God has assigned us . . . Neither do we go beyond our limits"* (2 Corinthians 10:13, 15, NIV).

FIRING DECISIONS

Most Christians in business are confused about the responsibility of employers to their employees. Many employers believe they should never dismiss an employee for fear it would reflect badly on their commitment to Christ. Many Christian employees believe that because they work for a Christian they should be guaranteed permanent employment regardless of their performance.

On the other hand, some Christian employers treat their employees badly. They are unkind and even harsh, damaging the cause of Christ in the process.

Malcolm was such a person. He owned a construction company that employed 400. Malcolm talked often about his faith in Christ and gave generously to Christian causes. He believed himself to be a fair man but refused to accept advice from others.

He also was extremely moody. At a meeting, he might ask for the opinions of his management team and appear to appreciate them. But then after the meeting he might fire a manager whose input he perceived as critical.

Malcolm often attempted to bring Christ into his business. He tried having company devotion times, sending employees to seminars, giving away Bibles, but nothing worked.

Malcolm's company contracted with the Navy to make parts for a new fighter aircraft. The contract would double the business, but it also carried stiff penalties for defective workmanship. Things went well for several months. Then, unexpectedly, the Navy rejected some defective parts. They told Malcolm that the parts would have to be re-fabricated at his cost, and if it happened again, the contract would be canceled.

In a fit of rage, Malcolm told the plant manager to fire Johnson, the supervisor of the shift responsible for producing the defective parts. Johnson had been with the company for years and was recognized as their best supervisor.

Within an hour, the plant manager and the entire crew working for Johnson submitted the following resignation: "We all quit. We won't work for a hypocrite like Mr. Self-Righteous. We would rather keep our integrity than work for a hypocrite who talks about God and then fires a decent man who's going through what Johnson's going through!"

The plant manager explained to Malcolm, "We know the company is more important to you than people, but Johnson's wife and daughter both have terminal cancer, and he has to care for his young twin boys. He's been driving a hundred miles each evening to visit his wife and daughter at the hospital. His medical bills are nearly $200,000. He hasn't used his sick leave because he'll need it when his wife becomes incapacitated. He has worked weekends without pay to keep his paperwork up-to-date so the contract wouldn't be jeopardized. And in the middle of all this, you fired him! You wonder why more of the employees don't come to your devotionals and the other Christian activities? It's because your actions speak louder than your words, and they don't want anything to do with it."

BIBLICAL PRINCIPLES FOR FIRING

Acting fairly and humanely toward employees is one of the most important responsibilities of an employer. But an employee's responsibility to an employer is also important. When an employee refuses to conform to company rules, dismissal may be necessary.

As difficult as it is for people when they lose their jobs, you are not doing them any favors by retaining them when they should be fired. If you have been diligent to correct problems, and employees are unable or unwilling to respond positively, you are doing them a disservice by keeping them. If they have made poor career choices, the sooner they make a change, the sooner they can flourish. If they have character flaws, the flaws need to be corrected.

What does the Bible say about firing? Let's start by defining the prerequisites any godly owner or manager must meet before the dismissal of an employee should be considered.

1. Have a clearly defined job description.
2. Develop a clearly defined set of job standards: time, dress, expected performance.
3. Communicate your expectations clearly in writing.
4. Communicate your dissatisfactions clearly and quickly in writing.
5. Have a trial correction period.

Before getting into the details of how to handle a dismissal, let's examine two of the points that most businesspeople violate: communicating expectations and dissatisfactions.

THE NEED TO COMMUNICATE

Too often, an owner or manager allows grievances to build until they become intolerable; then they unload on an unsuspecting employee who should have been corrected long before. It is vitally important to communicate early and clearly.

Peter needed a field supervisor for his commercial plumbing business. At a Bible study, a friend mentioned that his son, Brad, was looking for a job. Brad had worked summers for Peter while in college and had proven to be a quick learner and natural leader.

Peter hired Brad to be his field supervisor. Peter was excited when Brad suggested that he could organize a Bible study at the job sites and perhaps lead some of the men to Christ.

At first, it went well. Brad made a good impression on the work crews and spent most of his time getting to know the men. But then Peter realized that Brad was spending too much time with the men who were having problems, and his Bible studies were lasting too long.

Instead of honestly confronting the issue, Peter merely "suggested" that perhaps some of the studies should be limited to 15 minutes. Brad interpreted this to mean that he should take the matter under consideration, but since great things were happening at the studies and lives were being changed, he decided against cutting the meetings short. Then construction workers from other companies began seeking Brad's counsel. He hardly had time to fill out the necessary reports.

Peter decided to take the coward's way out. He planned to fire Brad on the pretext that he couldn't afford his salary. Peter began the conversation by saying, "Brad, I need to talk to you about your job. How do you think it's going so far?"

Since Peter was so discouraged with Brad, he assumed that Brad was feeling the same way. He was shocked when Brad answered, "I think it's going great, sir. I believe we're right on target."

Peter stammered, "What?" Then he asked, "Tell me what your job is, Brad. What are you doing?"

Brad looked a little confused, but he replied, "Well, I assumed that you want me to share Christ with the men at the construction sites."

Peter was amazed. "But, don't you realize that I hired you to oversee the jobs themselves and that your evangelism and Bible studies are interfering with the work?"

Now it was Brad's turn to be shocked. "No, I really didn't know that's what you were expecting. Why, you must think I've been wasting company money and time."

Peter realized that God had called Brad to be an evangelist in the work place, so he asked three other business owners to help fund Brad's salary. Today he is a well-known business evangelist.

Many business people make Peter's mistake. They wrongly assume that they have expressed the job expectations clearly. To avoid making that common error, we are better off to over-communicate to make sure that job expectations and evaluations are fully understood.

It is wise to provide applicants with written job descriptions. Ask the applicant to read the description carefully and then explain to you what it means.

Another important principle is to *never* let the sun go down on a problem without making a commitment to handle it. If the issue is very emotional and we risk saying something we would regret later, it's a good idea to allow a little time to pass to cool down—perhaps hours rather than days. If we wait too long, we usually will not deal with the problem and it continues to worsen.

DISMISSAL

The same basic principle applies when it is the people themselves that are the problem—people problems almost never get better when left alone. In time, the problems usually compound. The Lord told us, *"A little leaven leavens the whole lump"* (Galatians 5:9). When you allow dissenters, thieves or slackers to continue uncorrected, others are encouraged to follow their example.

REASONS FOR DISMISSAL
The following list, although not exhaustive, contains the most common biblically justifiable reasons for dismissing an employee.

1. Dishonesty
The Lord requires honesty. *"You shall not steal nor deal falsely nor lie to one another"* (Leviticus 19:11). In Matthew 9:13, God reveals that He wants us to *"desire compassion"* toward others. We should lean more toward forgiveness than seeking retribution for sins against us. In business, we believe this means that we should forgive people who are repentant for their misconduct and show evidence of truly wishing to change. This does not mean overlooking or simply tolerating dishonesty; that becomes an unintentional encouragement of it. *"If a ruler pays attention to falsehood, all his ministers become wicked"* (Proverbs 29:12).

The manager of a sporting goods store was an excellent salesman but an ineffective manager. The store employed outside salespeople who did a lot of wholesale business with schools.

The owner required the salespeople to sign for samples of athletic equipment they took from the warehouse, but the manager never enforced this rule. As a result, most of the equipment was never checked out.

This lax attitude about sales samples influenced other employees who began to pilfer. The problem grew to alarming proportions when the annual audit revealed a loss of nearly $50,000 in inventory.

One of the employees was caught selling company goods along the roadside. His excuse was, "I thought it was okay since nobody cared how much stock we took out."

It is management's responsibility to enforce policies that reduce such temptations. That includes firing employees who break these rules. First, we must be sure that the standard for acceptable and unacceptable conduct is clear to everyone. Then, if a theft is discovered, we should decisively confront the issue with anyone who is involved.

Employee dishonesty often involves such issues as misuse of the company telephone, equipment, or supplies. In these cases, confronting the dishonesty may be all that is necessary. If the confrontation is done with an attitude of caring, and the goal is to restore the individual, this action can be a positive witness for the Lord.

However, if the offense involves blatant theft of money or materials, a more serious consequence is in order. It is always important that the punishment fit the crime.

2. Disobedience

There are many degrees of employee disobedience. Open rebellion is simple to spot and relatively simple to deal with; the employee either stops rebelling or is asked to leave the company. Subtle disobedience, however, is more difficult to identify and infinitely more difficult to control.

Allen's company employed a secretary who, although very good at her job, had a habit of undercutting the authority of her supervisor. She was careful never to cross the line of open rebellion, but her subtle remarks were poison. She made comments to other staff such as, "I heard that Julie can't be fired. It makes you wonder why, doesn't it?"

She also began generally stirring up dissension and quietly accusing management of violating the Fair Labor Standards Act that governs hourly employees. Allen finally decided to handle the situation by meeting with the others who were involved, explaining to them the problem of the secretary's behavior. Once they began to see her pattern, they made it a practice to call into the discussion any other people she was talking about; then they would ask her to repeat what she had just told them. Within a few weeks she resigned.

3. Laziness

The Lord requires us to work hard. *"Whatever your hand finds to do, do it with all your might"* (Ecclesiastes 9:10, NIV). *"The precious possession of a man is diligence"* (Proverbs 12:27). In Scripture, hard work and diligence are encouraged; laziness is condemned. *"He who is slack in his work is brother to him who destroys"* (Proverbs 18:9).

Paul's life was an example of hard work. *"With labor and hardship we kept working night and day so that we might not be a burden to any of you . . . in order to offer ourselves as a model for you, that you might follow our example"* (2 Thessalonians 3:8-9).

Unfortunately, there is a clear trend toward laziness in our society. Therefore, it is especially important to establish policies that promote hard work and choose employees accordingly. Then, you need to discipline those who are not faithful.

General George Patton had a problem with lazy parachute packers in World War II. Several pilots died when their chutes didn't open because of sloppy packing. A parachute inspection found that 30 percent were improperly packed.

General Patton quickly solved the problem. He charged into the parachute-packing depot and commanded all the packers to take the last chutes they had packed and come with him. He herded them into an aircraft and had them jump, wearing the chutes they had just packed. He continued this practice for the remainder of the war and never had a packing problem again.

Efforts should be made to motivate slothful employees. If, after reasonable efforts have been made without change, the only solution may be to remove the problem employee.

4. Incompetence

One of the most difficult situations from a Christian perspective is that of a cooperative but incompetent employee. Allowing people to remain in positions that they are clearly incapable of handling is a disservice to them and the company. But before dismissing incompetent employees, you should first determine if they have been placed in inappropriate positions. Sometimes a change in job responsibilities can solve the problem.

Doctor Jerry Greer hired Nancy, a registered nurse, to work in his office. Her job was to interview patients and prepare them for their appointment. She was also frequently required to give shots and take blood. Unfortunately, she was completely inept at handling shots and blood.

During her first week on the job, Nancy gave a patient the wrong shot, incorrectly labeled two blood samples and two patient charts. Nancy was so disorganized that Jerry soon learned he could never entrust any important tasks to her. Each time he talked to her about her shortcomings, Nancy was pleasant and apologetic.

Jerry's dilemma: what to do with this sweet but highly inefficient nurse. Finally, he asked her, "Nancy, why did you become a nurse?"

"Because I really want to help people," she replied. "I like working with people."

Jerry asked, "If you could do what your heart really desires, what would it be?"

"Oh, I'd love to work with older people in a nursing home," she answered as her face lit up. "I helped my grandmother while she was alive, and I really enjoyed it."

Jerry knew a doctor who owned a large nursing home and had mentioned the problems of getting nurses to work in elderly care because of the long hours. Jerry called him about Nancy.

The nursing home owner hired Nancy and was thrilled with her performance. He discovered that she was dyslexic, and he assigned a student helper to handle Nancy's details. Nancy had a tremendous impact on the patients because of her genuine affection for them.

Maintaining people in jobs for which they are neither qualified nor motivated is a disservice to both the company and the employees, yet many Christians do so out of a misguided sense of ethics.

STEPS FOR DISMISSAL

Now that we have considered the reasons for dismissal, we suggest taking the following steps prior to dismissing any employee.

1. Institute a trial correction period.

When you realize that you must take disciplinary action and that dismissal may be necessary, first give the employee an opportunity to change. Establish a trial correction period and tell the employee the exact purpose for the trial: It is a precursor to more punitive action. Detail the minimum requirements in writing and document the meeting in the employee's personnel file.

If the trial period is longer than 30 days, there should be at least two additional face-to-face reviews during the period.

2. Conduct an exit interview.

If the employee does not improve sufficiently, the immediate manager should meet with the employee to discuss the necessity of dismissal. Once you reach the end of the process and decide to dismiss, complete it quickly and require the employee to leave the business environment.

Provide adequate compensation in the form of severance or extended pay and, if appropriate, assist the terminated employee to secure other employment.

3. Provide job referrals.

Assuming that the dismissal did not result from a problem that would prohibit a future job referral, the exit interview should include providing a letter of recommendation and perhaps even the offer of assistance in locating another job. Remember, the fact that someone did not work out for your company in a particular position does not necessarily mean a mismatch somewhere else.

REASONS TO ABORT A DISMISSAL ACTION

You may sometimes find it necessary to reverse your decision to dismiss an employee. Being a Christian employer involves compassion as well as discipline.

There are several reasons why a dismissal action might be aborted. Remember, any action taken by a godly employer should always be done in a spirit of love and concern for the others involved. The damage that an angry, vengeful employer can do is sometimes irreparable. *"There is one who speaks rashly like the thrusts of a sword, but the tongue of the wise brings healing"* (Proverbs 12:18).

1. The employee meets the conditions of the trial period.

This may seem too obvious to mention, but if you establish trial periods for employees to improve and they meet your conditions, don't dismiss them. Unfortunately, some employers dismiss anyway because of pride or hurt feelings; for them, the trial period was simply a formality to satisfy the federal Fair Labor Standards Act.

It takes wisdom to admit a mistake—especially if you're the boss. Some employers are so proud they would never admit an error in judgment. Employees don't think less of an authority who admits a wrong. They respect and admire that person all the more.

2. The employee shows a repentant attitude.

In a dialogue with Jesus, Peter asked, *"'Lord, how often shall my brother sin against me and I forgive him? Up to seven times?' Jesus said to him, 'I do not say to you, up to seven times, but up to seventy times seven'"* (Matthew 18:21-22). The principle behind the Lord's reply was that we should go far beyond the requirements of society.

The same principle applies in business. If someone violates a company policy that merits dismissal but truly displays a repentant spirit, the dismissal should be set aside. Sometimes it can be difficult to discern whether a person is genuinely repentant or simply is sorry he or she was caught.

Leonard suspected he was being robbed by his company accountant. He initiated an audit and confirmed his suspicions. At first, the accountant denied everything, but she eventually confessed to pilfering small amounts that totaled approximately $1,200 from the petty cash fund.

Her dismissal was immediate; the question was whether to prosecute. After discussing the situation with her pastor, he decided not to prosecute since this was her first offense.

A few days later, she came to Leonard's office to ask his forgiveness. She offered to start paying the money back each month as she could. She also offered him a note that designated her car as collateral for the debt.

Leonard asked why she had stolen the money. She replied that her husband had left her, forcing her to be the sole provider for herself and their five children. At first, she had only borrowed the money with the intention of repaying it from her next paycheck, but eventually she got in so far that she couldn't pay what she had taken. She had stopped the pilfering several weeks earlier and wanted to confess several times but didn't for fear of losing her job.

Leonard offered her the job back again with the agreement that the money would be repaid from her salary at the rate of $100 a month. In the meantime, he went to her pastor and worked out a way to help meet her budget through the church without her knowing it. She continued to work as a valued employee and never repeated the offense. Forgiveness was the correct procedure in her case.

3. You discover outside mitigating circumstances.

Outside pressures can influence people to act in ways that are uncharacteristic of them. When confronted with disapproval, many people will blame outside factors in an attempt to avoid responsibility. Although everyone is exposed to outside pressures, those pressures can't all be allowed to affect job performance. But under extreme duress, people will often change their behavior. Allow the benefit of the doubt if the behavior is unusual for them—especially if they have been faithful in the past.

People in these circumstances are commonly dismissed, and in some cases it is necessary. First, however, make an effort to understand the outside circumstances. Too few businesspeople apply the principle: *"A friend loves at all times, and a brother is born for adversity"* (Proverbs 17:17).

DISMISSAL SUMMARY

When in doubt about what to do, lean heavily on God's wisdom, and show mercy. When you must dismiss an employee, carry it out in an attitude of love and concern. Mercy means being concerned about the financial needs of anyone in your employment, even ex-employees. Be sensitive to God's leading about helping those you dismiss, even when you dismiss them for a valid reason.

PAY DECISIONS

Ron owned a manufacturing plant with 200 employees, most of them assembly-line workers. Women filled most of these positions because of the great attention to detail that was required; and women worked for less than men because their income was often supplemental.

The difficulty was that some of the women on the assembly line were single parents who were the sole supporters of their families. Jennifer was a 34-year-old mother of three whose ex-husband refused to support his family. Jennifer worked hard and was a valued employee, but her minimum-wage job just wouldn't meet all the bills. She never complained, but on two occasions the claims court had issued a garnishment on her wages.

Ron asked her about the latest garnishment. "Jennifer, I received a note from the small claims court that we must garnish your wages for a car accident. Don't you carry liability insurance?"

"I used to, but I just couldn't afford to renew the policy. I'm really sorry, Sir. Will this cost me my job?"

"No, Jennifer," Ron replied. "You're a good worker and I want to help if I can. Would you be willing to see a financial counselor who may be able to help you manage your money a little better? If you keep driving without insurance, you'll lose your license."

"I'll be happy to talk with anyone. If I lose my license, I don't know how I'll get to work."

Ron knew that Jennifer's value to the company was worth paying for her car insurance, but the union that represented the workers would never agree to his giving her a bonus or a raise without doing the same for everyone else. He wanted to raise her pay because she needed the money, but he couldn't.

The next week Jennifer's counselor called Ron. He told Ron that Jennifer was a good money manager who simply didn't make enough to cover her expenses. "In fact," he said, "it will take another $125 a month just to buy the necessities for her family."

Since Jennifer didn't attend a church, Ron decided to give the money to his church and ask the church to assist with Jennifer's bills under the counselor's supervision. For three years, Ron continued to supplement Jennifer's income. She joined the church. Eventually she moved into a supervisory position with a salary adequate to meet her family's needs.

BIBLICAL PRINCIPLES FOR PAYING EMPLOYEES

The Lord is serious about paying a fair wage. *"I will draw near to you for judgment; and I will be a swift witness against . . . those who oppress the wage earner in his wages . . . says the Lord"* (Malachi 3:5). And James 5:4 says, *"Behold, the pay of the laborers who mowed your fields, and which has been withheld by you, cries out against you; and the outcry of those who did the harvesting has reached the ears of the Lord."* Many Christian businesspeople violate this principle in their businesses.

We believe the Scripture teaches:

1. God does not require that everybody be paid the same amount.
2. Those who do better work should be paid more.
3. God demands fairness in paying employees.
4. An employer has a responsibility to meet the minimum needs of the employees.

Each of these conclusions raises other questions. What really constitutes someone's minimum needs? How can you reward extra effort in a union environment? What is "fair" when it comes to paying people? Should you reward loyalty?

We don't pretend to have all the answers to these questions, but we can identify some relevant principles.

1. Defining minimum needs

Defining the need level of another person is not simple. One person may consider a microwave oven a need, but someone else may struggle to have one good meal a day. What someone in a third-world country considers a luxury may be viewed as a bare necessity in America.

One of the most helpful ways to determine other people's needs is simply to put yourself in their position and see if you could live on what they are earning. If employers would do this, many would admit they aren't paying a fair wage.

Nothing in the Bible says that we should all make the same wage or that owners can't earn more than their workers. But the Bible does speak against cheating the workers of what is due them. *"Woe to him who builds his house without righteousness and his upper rooms without justice, who uses his neighbor's services without pay and does not give him his wages"* (Jeremiah 22:13).

Dean hired Big Joe as a printer for his company. Big Joe had a large family and was not able to care properly for their needs on his income. He was poorly educated and would not be able earn more than Dean was paying him. He was cooperative but unskilled.

Dean was deeply committed to Christ. As he thought about Big Joe's situation, Dean felt that the Lord was asking him to give Big Joe a raise despite the company's tight finances. Dean had no idea how God was going to provide the income, but by faith he gave Big Joe a raise of $500 a month. It was a huge encouragement to Dean to see the Lord faithfully increase his business as he cared about the needs of his staff.

Many people create their own problems by overspending, but some are clearly underpaid. If I place myself in an employee's position and cannot find a way to make the available money stretch to meet his or her minimum needs, then I may be paying too little.

2. Situational economics

Is it fair to replace long-term employees with younger, lower-paid workers? Few business philosophies are more reflective of the motives of those in authority than *situational economics*.

A company may have many loyal and dependable long-time employees. They usually earn higher wages than new employees. Pure economics would dictate replacing them with new, lower-paid employees.

This approach is not biblical. *"Do not let kindness and truth leave you; bind them around your neck, write them on the tablet of your heart. So you will find favor and good repute in the sight of God and man"* (Proverbs 3:3-4).

A godly person displays kindness and justice in business, and the practice of dumping long-term employees is neither kind nor just. Other problems surface when company loyalty is compromised.

Robert operated his textile company according to the situational economics principle—he took every advantage the economy provided. At the time, the economy was slow, jobs were scarce and employees were plentiful. He replaced many of his higher-paid people with cheaper labor. To avoid violating union rules, he did this through selective shift assignments and shutdowns. Robert, a Christian, rationalized his actions as logical for the times.

Two years later, the economy picked up and the textile business came under intense foreign pressure. Within a few months the carpet industry plunged into the deepest recession since the Great Depression. Business was down and raw material prices skyrocketed. Robert appealed to the union for wage concessions and a short-term loan to save his company. His employees rejected both, saying they would rather lose their jobs than help.

The company was dissolved and sold for partial settlement of the outstanding debts. Robert filed for personal bankruptcy.

If owners sow kindness and genuine care, that is what they will later reap.

Few business philosophies are more reflective of the motives of those in authority than situational *economics.*

HUMAN RESOURCES NOTES

3. The power of reward

Many employers are quick to criticize but slow to reward good performance—either with praise or with money.

"The guy I work for never thanks me for anything I do," Susan declared. "I can do 99 percent of the work perfectly, and he'll always criticize the one percent that's not perfect."

"That's really too bad," Sheri replied, thinking of her own boss, Mr. Rhone. He always demanded her very best but made a point of complimenting her work before correcting her errors.

Her first day on the job, her boss said, "This is your first real job out of high school, and I'd like to help you get started right. I'll correct your work if I see something that needs improvement, but I'll always try to do it constructively." Three months later, he gave Sheri a sizable raise and praised her efforts.

Mr. Rhone often corrected her work, but he had proven his concern for her. As a result, she developed into an efficient, confident secretary.

Sheri hadn't always felt secure, even at home. Her father, also a successful businessman and a Christian, had always used his position to rule people rather than lead them. Sheri had secretly feared that maybe God was like that, and she had even stopped going to church. But in Mr. Rhone she had a different example of a Christian employer: firm but fair. He encouraged Sheri by saying, "Remember Proverbs 22:29: *'Do you see a man skilled in his work? He will stand before kings; he will not stand before obscure men.'* That will carry you a long way. You may have bosses who won't recognize your hard work, but they're the exception. Remember that the best testimony for Christ is to love others and be excellent in your work."

4. Rewarding different abilities

Each of us is equipped to do at least one thing well. Sometimes that ability pays well and sometimes it doesn't. There is nothing unscriptural about maintaining different rates of pay. *"To one he gave five talents* [a talent was a sum of money], *to another, two, and to another, one, each according to his own ability"* (Matthew 25:15). For example, a top-producing salesperson may earn more than the sales manager. A gifted Information Technology person may be paid more than a bookkeeper.

5. Rewarding loyalty

Loyalty can be defined as "a commitment to a person or company, even in the face of adversity." By that definition, loyalty is rare today. When you discover an employee displaying loyalty, do everything in your power to reward it.

God's Word supports honoring those who are loyal. Throughout the Bible there are dozens of examples of God rewarding loyalty and punishing unfaithfulness. What is it worth to have employees who are loyal and think the best, rather than the worst, of your decisions? Anyone who has ever worked around disloyal employees can answer that. It's worth a lot.

A Christian ministry leader found himself in the middle of a scandal created by a member of his family. He had nothing to do with the wrongdoing;

his only error had been refusing to listen to the rumors about his relative until it was too late to correct the situation privately. When the scandal broke, the majority of this man's staff revolted and demanded his resignation. He was devastated by these people he had believed to be loyal.

Fortunately, a pastor who knew him well remained loyal, believing he had done nothing wrong. This pastor assumed temporary control of the organization. He allowed staff members to express their concerns but refused to consider accusations that were unsupported by witnesses or verifiable facts.

After days of interaction with the staff without finding any convicting evidence, the pastor called them together. He said, "I have examined the accusations and found nothing of substance." Then he drew a line on the floor and said, "Everyone who is loyal to him step over this line. Everyone who isn't willing to support him stay where you are."

The group was split evenly between those who stepped over and those who did not. To the latter he said, "Please see the accountant for your severance pay on your way out."

The evidence that God was in that decision is still being confirmed by the changed lives of those who are touched by this leader's teaching. If you have it in your power to pay loyal people more, do so. If it is not in your power, find some other way to show them how much you value their loyalty.

 SUGGESTED RESOURCES

Personality Testing

Career Direct®
Crown Financial Ministries
(The *Career Direct®* Guidance System helps individuals find their God-given design. It profiles personality, interests, skills, and values and instantly generates over 30 pages of individualized reports. Order from Crown at 1-800-722-1976 or Crown.org.)

Character Development

Character First
Characterfirst.com

Discipleship

The Master Plan of Evangelism
by Robert Coleman
Fleming H. Revel Co.

1. People are a business's most valuable asset. Carefully and prayerfully hiring the right person is critical.

2. Promote people who have been faithful employees and who possess the ability to handle greater leadership.

3. Use a written job description and make certain you have communicated your job expectations clearly.

4. A Christian employer may terminate an employee for lack of satisfactory job performance, dishonesty, laziness, and other similar factors.

5. Pay employees a fair wage.

HUMAN RESOURCES NOTES

ORGANIZATION

*"Do not be bound together with unbelievers;
for what partnership have righteousness and lawlessness,
or what fellowship has light with darkness?"*
2 Corinthians 6:14

ORGANIZATION HOMEWORK

Homework to be completed for Chapter 6

Before attending class complete the:
☐ Scripture to Memorize
☐ Organization Homework

 SCRIPTURE TO MEMORIZE

"Do not be bound together with unbelievers; for what partnership have righteousness and lawlessness, or what fellowship has light with darkness?" (2 Corinthians 6:14)

DAY ONE – REVIEW CHAPTER 5

Read the Human Resources Notes on pages 74-90 and answer.

1. What in the Notes was particularly helpful or challenging?

2. How will you apply what you learned to your personal and business life?

DAY TWO – CORE VALUES AND TEAMWORK

1. Have you documented in writing the values (core values) for your business that you will not compromise under any circumstances? If so, list the most important core values.

2. Do you have a strategy to use teamwork effectively in your business? (Even if you operate a one-person business, you will need to work with vendors, referral sources, etc.) If so, please describe it.

DAY THREE – BUSINESS PARTNERSHIPS

1. What are the most common reasons for creating a business partnership?

Read 2 Corinthians 6:14-15. *"Do not be bound together with unbelievers; for what partnership have righteousness and lawlessness, or what fellowship has light with darkness? Or what harmony has Christ with Belial, or what has a believer in common with an unbeliever?"*

2. How can you apply the principle in this passage to business partnerships?

3. Have you been in a business partnership? If so, what has your experience been?

ORGANIZATION HOMEWORK

1. If you consider forming a partnership or privately held corporation with a person who knows Christ, what issues do you think you need to agree upon before entering into the partnership or corporation?

2. If you are married, describe how you would involve your spouse in this decision.

3. What personal character qualities would a potential partner or closely held stockholder need to have?

4. How should you document your agreement with a potential partner or stockholder?

5. Describe your agreement if a partner or stockholder wishes to leave the partnership or corporation. Do you have a buy-sell agreement?

Read Ephesians 6:2-3. *"Honor your father and mother (which is the first commandment with a promise), so that it may be well with you, and that you may live long on the earth."*

6. What adjustments would you make in your Day Three answers if you were dealing with family members?

7. If you are in an existing partnership with your parents (and they do not yet know the Lord), how do you seek to honor them in the partnership?

DAY FIVE – FORM OF BUSINESS

Read Ephesians 6:5-6. *"Slaves* [employees], *obey your earthly masters* [employers] *with respect and fear, and with sincerity of heart, just as you would obey Christ"* (NIV).

1. Do you think that an employer-employee relationship with a non-Christian violates the principle of not being bound together? Why or why not?

2. Describe the form of your business (sole proprietorship, partnership, or corporation).

3. Describe the personal benefits as well as the disadvantages you have experienced using this form of ownership.

Note: You may read the Organization Notes prior to completing this Day Six Homework if you wish.

CASE STUDY

Luke Allison, a committed Christian, owned a real estate company in a community with a changing business climate. He served a bedroom community of 120,000 people, many of whom worked in the neighboring city. The home sales market was very slow.

Maintaining an independent firm was basic to his approach to business. However, he was losing market share to the large national realtors who had moved into his town. These national firms were not only attracting buyers but also his salespeople.

A respected long-term realtor in the community suggested a business venture to Luke. They would merge the two businesses and together attract experienced salespeople who did not prefer a large national company. This would stabilize their business and provide them the opportunity to expand into the major metropolitan market as well.

Analysis

1. Define the problem/issue.

2. Identify the people involved.

3. Identify special circumstances and potential consequences.

4. What actions do you think should be taken? Why?

5. How would God be honored and glorified by these actions?

Application

Based on this case study and what you have learned from the Organization lesson, please answer the following questions.

1. What insight have you gained concerning your business?

2. What changes might you need to make in the operation of your business?

3. What results would you hope to see?

PRACTICAL APPLICATION

Analyze the ownership of your existing business or the business you are contemplating. Describe what changes, if any, you need to make.

ORGANIZATION NOTES 👑

Please complete the Organization Homework (Days 1-5) before reading these notes.

Red Lobster had become a well-known national restaurant chain by the time the founder sold out to giant General Mills. During the next several years, Red Lobster's performance began to slide as customer satisfaction and store sales suffered while employee turnover increased.

The founder repurchased Red Lobster and installed a new leadership team. One of the first steps they took was to identify the organization's **core values**. They printed a booklet of their core values, and everyone in the organization read one of the values before each meeting. When the CEO met with the president, they read a core value. When a restaurant manager met with the servers, they read a core value. Red Lobster turned around in two years.

CORE VALUES OF YOUR BUSINESS

Core values are the basic principles by which you operate— the values you will not compromise under any circumstances.

Core values are the basic principles by which you operate—the values you will not compromise under any circumstance. Defining and reducing them to writing should be a priority, whether you are a one-person business or employ thousands. If you have a leadership team, it is wise to involve them in the process.

Settling on your list of core value is more than a simple brainstorming exercise. Give it the thought and discussion time it deserves; you will discover a new clarity in the purpose and unique personality of your business.

Your core values should permeate the culture of your business, influencing the way you relate to staff, customers, vendors—everyone in every phase of your operation. When you interview people for possible employment or when you consider a close working relationship or partnership, request that they study your core values. Those who share your values will be attracted; others will be repelled.

The purposes for documenting your core values are to:

- Clarify God's mission for your business.
- Help you maintain focus on the manner in which God wants you to perform your business.
- Promote unity in the business and help new members understand its culture.

To review Crown's core values, visit **Crown.org/Business**.

The remainder of this chapter will address teamwork and organizational issues. If you are a one-person organization, these principles may not seem applicable to your business at this time. However, many of them will apply to your affiliation with churches, associations, and other organizations. Also, understanding these principles will be crucial if you ever consider starting a business, if you counsel someone contemplating such a step, or if you enter into a close alliance with another business.

TEAMWORK

Earlier in the study, we discussed the value of a team of people working together: *"Two are better than one because they have a good return for their labor. For if either of them falls, the one will lift up his companion. But woe to the one who falls when there is not another to lift him up. Furthermore, if two lie down together they keep warm, but how can one be warm alone? And if one can overpower him who is alone, two can resist him. A cord of three strands is not quickly torn apart"* (Ecclesiastes 4:9-12).

Teams have the potential for exceptional results when there is a clear, common, and compelling purpose. This is true for large companies; it is also true for one-person firms. For example, almost every business needs solid relationships with vendors, referral sources, accountants, and the like.

Four principles foster the development of high-performance work teams. These principles help involve and empower everyone in the group, enhancing cooperation and freeing the leader to spend more time on higher-level functions.

1. Common purpose
There is no substitute for the team understanding its purpose and each member aligning to the purpose. The task of any team is to accomplish a stated, written objective and to strive to execute it with excellence. The purpose must be of sufficient importance to motivate the members to invest the necessary effort to accomplish it well.

2. Clear roles
Roles are simply a means of dividing the work of the team. All members must have a clear understanding of their own roles as well as those of other members, particularly those to whom they relate. Along with defining roles, teams must establish the processes they will use for managing meetings, making decisions, and pursuing other activities necessary to accomplish the mission.

3. Competent leadership
Effective leaders keep the team on task and encourage individual initiative and creativity.

4. Communication
No team can move faster than it communicates. Resolving communication breakdowns or bottlenecks may require a revision in standard operating pro-

cedures or an investment in newer technology. Efforts to improve operational effectiveness will have only marginal success if the speed and clarity of communication are not addressed first.

If your business is not already employing teams that are empowered by these four principles, consider investing the effort it will take to create them. One of your biggest jobs as a leader is to use resources available to you for maximum effectiveness. Empowered teams add value to each member's performance, creating a whole that is greater than the sum of its parts.

ORGANIZATION

The organizational structure of your business has a lot to do with its success. Every business leader faces important daily decisions. In reality, these decisions begin even before the business gets off the ground. Unfortunately, many entrepreneurs have forged ahead in their enthusiasm for a new venture without answering some key questions.

- Should I have a partner?
- Who should be in control?
- Should I incorporate?
- Am I liable if the business fails?
- Who will take over if I die?
- How can I keep my spouse informed concerning the business?

Each of these questions can be answered with help from God's Word. If you are already in the middle of operating a business, you may need to reassess some earlier assumptions.

Businesspeople incorporate or enter into partnerships for two basic reasons: to raise capital and to bring expertise or labor to a business. Additionally, a corporation and some types of partnerships create a shield from liability.

PARTNERSHIPS

Partnerships can be enormously successful. They can bring together people who have complementary skills and experience as well as needed capital.

What scriptural principles guide the formation of a partnership? The question, "What is a partnership?" can be answered best by examining the definition of a yoke, which was used as an illustration by the apostle Paul in 2 Corinthians 6:14-15. *"Do not be yoked together with unbelievers. For what do righteousness and wickedness have in common? Or what fellowship can light have with darkness? What harmony is there between Christ and Belial? What does a believer have in common with an unbeliever?"* (NIV).

Paul instructed believers not to be yoked (bound) together with nonbelievers. He described the bond of partnership with the Greek word *zugo*, meaning a yoke used to bind two animals together for the purpose of pulling a burden.

"Do not be yoked together with unbelievers. For what do righteousness and wickedness have in common? . . . What does a believer have in common with an unbeliever?" (2 Corinthians 6:14-15, NIV).

In Paul's generation, this yoke was the perfect example of an equal partnership. Animals were paired carefully because of the burden they would share. If one animal was larger than the other, the heavy yoke would not be carried evenly. There had to be a lead animal, but there could be only one. If both oxen tended toward being the lead animal, they would struggle for dominance and wear themselves out. If neither wanted to lead, they would wander off the track.

Being equally yoked means equal and balanced. In the business environment, the most common example is that of an equal partnership. In this arrangement, each of the partners is obligated by whatever agreements the other partner makes. So if one partner commits to a contract in the name of the partnership, all partners are committed.

1. Non-Christian partners

"Do not be bound together with unbelievers" (2 Corinthians 6:14). The logic behind the prohibition is to avoid conflicting values.

Ken, a committed Christian, graduated first in his class at law school. Although many top law firms recruited him, he decided to practice law in a small town in partnership with an attorney who did not know Christ but had a terrific reputation. Their personalities and talents complemented each other well, and the experienced partner became Ken's mentor. The firm enjoyed remarkable success.

Over time, however, it became apparent to Ken that his basic values and love for the things of God began to irritate his partner. Regardless of the partnership's financial success, Ken felt restrained in using the practice of law to promote the work of God. He finally decided the only solution was to leave.

Many Christians enter partnerships with nonbelievers because of economic necessity—not biblical principle. When such partnerships survive, it is often because the Christians have learned to compromise and are not committed to applying God's principles to their business.

2. Christian partners

We recommend that you be extremely careful before entering into a partnership—even with someone who knows Christ. We have seen far too many Christian partnerships end badly.

Be sure you know your potential partner well. Answer these questions:

- Does this person have an unquestioned integrity and commitment to Christ?
- Does this person consistently handle money according to God's principles?
- Does this person have a reasonable lifestyle?
- If this person is married, is the spouse in favor of the partnership? Is the spouse a person of integrity?

Another important question: Is this person as hard working as I am? In our experience, a partnership will not survive if one of the equal partners contributes much more to the success of the partnership than the other.

Many Christians enter partnerships with nonbelievers because of economic necessity—not biblical principle. When such partnerships survive, it is often because the Christians have learned to compromise and are not committed to applying God's principles to their business.

3. Is the other partner a likely candidate for God's discipline?

When we form a partnership or a corporation of equal ownership with others, we link our economic futures. You don't want to hitch your wagon to someone who is likely to incur God's discipline because of violating Scripture. Your association will result in your suffering as well.

Harold and Thomas were equal owners of a real-estate development company that enjoyed remarkable profitability over a period of three years. Harold maintained a reasonable standard of living and remained focused on putting Christ first in his life and business. Thomas, however, became enamored with his new wealth. He spent wildly, no longer attended church and completely walked away from Christ.

Harold told a friend, "I am afraid for Thomas, and I am afraid for myself. God loves Thomas and will undoubtedly seek to get his attention. Money has become Thomas's god. We are no longer equally yoked. I need to sell out to Thomas."

In his greed, Thomas was unwilling to pay Harold a fair price, but Harold sold anyway. Today, Thomas is almost bankrupt. Hebrews 12:6, 11 reads, *"Those whom the Lord loves He disciplines. . . . All discipline for the moment seems not to be joyful, but sorrowful."*

FAMILY PARTNERSHIPS

Family partnership can be extremely rewarding; they can also be gut-wrenching. These partnerships are particularly risky because of the possibility of long-term bruised relationships. Here are some of the potential challenges:

- Parents, assuming that their children want to come into the business, may exert undue pressure on them.
- Parents may lead in an autocratic style.
- There may be no succession plan—no exit strategy for the parents, and they hold on too long.
- Parents give ownership equally to all the children with no one in charge.

It is particularly important to commit family partnership agreements to writing. What about already-existing partnerships between a Christian and family members who don't know Christ? The principles in God's Word do not differentiate between family members and friends when it comes to partnerships. In existing partnerships, Christians should seek to remain as they are unless the relationship forces them to compromise their spiritual convictions.

If the unsaved partner is a father or mother, however, there are higher principles governing that relationship. *"God said, 'Honor your father and mother,' and, 'He who speaks evil of father or mother, let him be put to death'"* (Matthew 15:4). Thus, the principle of honoring our fathers and mothers is a command that must supersede the prohibition against being unequally yoked. Obviously, a Christian should not allow even a parent to force him or her to sin. Assuming that parents are not requiring you to sin, do not ask them to leave the business out of fear of being unequally yoked.

GUIDELINES FOR ASSESSING A PARTNERSHIP

Any Christian thinking about partnership should ask two fundamental questions: "Who is in charge?" and "Do we agree on fundamental values?"

1. Who is in charge?

This question is often ignored in the formative stages of a partnership out of fear of embarrassment. If the business just breaks even, it may not result in a problem. But if the business is very successful or fails, this issue will become central.

The power that comes from controlling a successful enterprise will test the commitment of the strongest Christian. If the issue of who is in charge is not settled up front, it can easily create a rift in the partnership.

Conversely, if the business gets into financial difficulty, strong, decisive leadership will be required to pull it out. Saving a business that is in trouble may mean laying off family members and restricting the outflow of money. For one equal partner to tell another that he or she has to go out and get a job because the business can't support them both is highly unlikely if the issue of control is not settled from the outset.

Richard was half-owner in an electronics-manufacturing firm. His partner, Gene, was a brilliant engineer who had developed several patented products that their company manufactured. The business was divided into two basic areas: research and development, under Gene's supervision; and sales and administration, under Richard's authority. The idea was to have equal but separate responsibilities.

In the third year, one of the products became very successful. For the first time they had the capital to move into a facility that would be adequate. Richard suddenly found himself arguing with his partner over whether to upgrade offices or buy additional test equipment for a new generation of products.

"But we've hardly scratched the surface on the sales of the last unit," Richard argued. "If we come out with another model right now, we'll kill the sales for the existing units. I suggest that we hold off on the development of the computerized version for a while. Besides, most of our customers don't need the computerized model. They don't have the volume to justify the additional cost."

"I want to start work on the new model," Gene said with a note of finality in his voice. "This business has been built on my designs so far, and now I finally have the funds to do some real research. I'm not going to spend my time redesigning hardware, Richard. I need to be working on new ideas. I know you'll find a market for them; don't worry about it. Maybe we'll redo the facility next year, after we've completed the design on this new line."

Richard realized that he was considered the lesser partner because of his lack of technical expertise. But he also realized that the best product in the world is worthless if it doesn't sell. And Gene was intent on pursuing his own interests, regardless of the need.

Looking back, Richard realized that they had avoided discussing any details of their partnership. Since they were both Christians, they had assumed

If the issue of who is in charge is not settled up front, it can easily create a rift in the partnership.

ORGANIZATION NOTES

they would be able to work out any difficulties as they came up. Now he was seeing another side of his partner. The business was simply a means for Gene to pursue his driving interest—the design and development of new equipment.

Richard had three basic choices: (1) quit the partnership, (2) fight for his rights as an equal partner, or (3) allow his partner to control the business. After praying about his decision and discussing it with his wife, Richard came to the conclusion that he should give a portion of his stock in the business to Gene, thus securing his partner's position as majority owner.

The next day when Gene came into his office, he found an envelope with one share of stock enclosed on his desk. He had assumed that Richard would fight him for control of the business. Staring at the stock certificate, he realized that Richard had done voluntarily what no court would have imposed upon him. He walked over to his new junior partner's office.

"Richard, why did you do this?" he asked.

"Well, I prayed about it, and Donna and I decided that either we believe what the Bible says or we don't. Philippians 2:3 says, *'Do nothing from selfishness or empty conceit, but with humility of mind let each of you regard one another as more important than himself.'* Since we know there can't be two heads of a business, I figured this would settle the issue. So you just tell me what you want me to do, and I'll do it."

Gene replied, "I guess I would like for you to pray with me, Richard. As you know, I've always had a problem with my pride."

Richard and Gene spent the next half-hour on their knees in prayer. This became their routine for as long as they were in business together. From that day on, Gene never attempted to mandate a decision on Richard. Instead, he would present his ideas and then ask for his partner's perspective. Without exception he followed Richard's lead in all business decisions, including the research and development budget. A larger company eventually purchased the business and made Richard the director of the marketing group and Gene the head of research and development. It just proves that *"The reward of humility and the fear of the Lord are riches, honor and life"* (Proverbs 22:4).

2. Confirm agreement on core values

Amos 3:3 underscores the need to agree on basic core values, *"Do two walk together unless they have agreed to do so?"* (NIV). Here are additional questions that you ought to answer:

- Are we committed to giving to the Lord's work and to charity from the business? If so, how much and to whom?
- Will we sue to collect debts?
- Will we hire family members in the business?
- Will we hire non-Christian employees? Managers?
- How many hours per week will we commit to work in the business?
- How much travel time away from home will we spend?
- Will we evangelize through the business?
- Have we executed a buy-sell agreement? How will it be funded?
- Will we sell the business at some future date?

- Have we clearly defined our respective responsibilities?
- Are we willing to be accountable to each other and to an outside group?

3. Put it in writing—Always

While there are very successful partnerships, many more fail than succeed. Crucial factors include their mutual commitment to the principles described in God's Word and their willingness to be open and honest with each other from the outset.

Approach any partnership with a high degree of caution. Unraveling one is usually heart wrenching. It is better to risk hurting someone's feelings up front by declining a proposed partnership than to devastate that person when the partnership fails.

If you can reach a mutually satisfactory agreement on a partnership, we strongly recommend that you write down every detail. It has been said that most of us will retain only 10 percent of what we hear after a month. Combine that with the fact that one person will often misunderstand what another says, and it is easy to see why so many business partners have difficulty sorting out their verbal agreements later.

The simplest way to resolve this problem is to draw up a written agreement and have all the parties sign it. Even so, there will be misunderstandings. If prospective partners are offended by your request to write out the total agreement, it is better to know their attitude in advance.

The reason Christians should always insist on putting things in writing is that we value relationships. We should put all agreements in writing in order to protect relationships from the inevitable misunderstandings that accompany verbal agreements. Put all of your agreements in writing, even the ones that are not legally binding documents such as the purpose and values statements.

CORPORATIONS

There was no such thing as a corporation when the Bible was written. However, in our opinion, it is biblically legitimate to incorporate. We recommend seeking competent legal and accounting advice to determine the advantages and disadvantages, including tax treatment, of the various types of corporations.

Today's use of the corporate shield to avoid personal liability for business losses is considered universally acceptable. But, is it really? In some instances, the use of the corporate shield is a blatant attempt to defraud; in others, it legitimately limits the liability of an innocent party.

Dominic Russo operated a small import/export business that specialized in office decor. He sold high-quality drapes and blinds from developing countries that were promoted by the U.S. government.

Dominic negotiated a large sale of window coverings to a national company for their home office subject to providing a fireproofing guarantee to meet local fire codes. He contacted his supplier's representatives and gave them the specifications he had been given. Within a week, the certification came back

We recommend seeking competent legal and accounting advice to determine the advantages and disadvantages, including tax treatment, of the various types of corporations.

along with the report from the foreign-based testing laboratory.

Using this data, the company completed their $150,000 purchase of window coverings, netting Dominic his largest single profit ever.

A few months later, a fire tore through the office buildings, the drapes contributing to its spread. Several people sustained injuries and later filed lawsuits for millions of dollars against the building's owner. The owner tested the window coverings and found that they not only failed the fireproofing requirements, they also emitted toxic fumes. He consequently filed suit against Dominic for his losses.

In court, Dominic presented evidence that he had relied on the data supplied by the foreign government agency representing the manufacturer. The government agency, when questioned, replied that the manufacturer was no longer in business and that it (the agency) refused all responsibility.

Dominic lost the lawsuit and was assigned damages of more than $15 million. This forced his company into bankruptcy because of its limited assets. He was spared the burden of this debt because the corporate shield prevented him from being sued personally. In this case, the corporate shield protected an innocent party.

STOCK OWNERSHIP

If someone buys a few shares in Microsoft or another large company, that person is not yoked together with those companies; he or she is purchasing only the right to an equitable distribution of dividends and a minority vote in company policies.

But what about a corporation owned by two people, each holding equal shares? If the intent is to create an equal sharing arrangement, then for the purposes of our discussion it is a partnership just as certainly as if the term *partnership* were used.

GOING PUBLIC

In the 1990s, the economy went through a period of rapid growth driven in part by startup technology companies. One young "dot-commer" became rich after the company's initial public offering (IPO). Reacting to a question from an interviewer about the ease with which he had gained his fortune, he retorted, "I deserved that money because I earned it! I worked hard at the company every day *for two years*!"

Some of those startups actually had good business plans and smart people running them. They went public and made millions of dollars. That's when their independent-thinking entrepreneurial leaders realized that everything had changed. They were no longer in control. After the IPO, it wasn't their company anymore, and they weren't free to make their own decisions. Investors now had a voice in running the company.

The advantage of an IPO is the additional capital it raises to grow the business and generously compensate the owners. The disadvantages include the enormous expense of conforming to public corporation regulations and the loss of freedom for the original owners to operate the company. There may be pressure from investors to compromise the biblical values the company was built upon. In many respects, the impact is similar to selling the company.

It is extremely important to seek experienced counsel before electing to go public. Evaluate your motives. Are you contemplating taking your company public simply to get rich quickly, or are there long-term advantages for the work of Christ?

OTHER ORGANIZATION ISSUES

1. Partnerships with limited liability

Several forms of partnership offer limited liability. Research the laws of your state to determine what options are available to you. The purpose of limited-liability partnerships is to allow individuals to invest in a business venture and acquire the tax benefits of a partnership without the liabilities of a full partnership.

In such a business relationship, individual investors are limited in their liability and sometimes in their authority. When a partnership has a managing partner, sometimes called the general partner, who retains total management authority of the business, we don't believe this constitutes a yoke.

2. Employer-employee relationship

Some Christians are concerned about working for unbelievers or having unbelievers working for them because of the prohibition against being unequally yoked. Such a relationship is not a yoke or partnership; one person is clearly the authority and the other, the subordinate. Unless Christian employees are forced to compromise their principles, there is no scriptural admonition against this type of authority relationship.

3. Influencing the organization

In today's highly secularized business world, for Christians to conduct their "Business By The Book" is a challenge. All godly businesspeople need fellowship with others of similar occupation, but none more than those in a very secular business environment. The businessperson who feels like a lone scout in enemy territory will rarely give much thought to really influencing the organization.

Christians in business need to influence the business and the industry in which they work. That can be difficult even if you are a sole proprietor. If you're working somewhere down the ladder in a secular corporation, it's doubly challenging. But that's where some of the most extraordinary things happen in people's lives. Where there is great darkness, a little light makes a big impact. When you are surrounded by those who do not know the Lord, simply living for Christ makes an enormous impression.

There is no better example of influencing an organization than the story of Daniel and his three friends. They were captured and led away in chains to Babylon, where they were trained in the ways of Babylonian culture to serve King Nebuchadnezzar. These four young men remained faithful to God in the

All godly businesspeople need fellowship with others of similar occupation, but none more than those in a very secular business environment.

midst of a pagan culture and in the end had an extraordinary impact on the Babylonian kingdom.

Their influence on Nebuchadnezzar and succeeding kings was certainly aided by some dramatic displays of God's power. *"God sent His angel and shut the lions' mouths"* (Daniel 6:22) to rescue Daniel from death in a lions' den. And the Lord protected Daniel's three friends when they were condemned to die in a fiery furnace. *"Blessed be God . . . who has sent His angel and delivered His servants who put their trust in Him"* (Daniel 3:28).

So how did they influence the nation without compromising their faith? These young men ascended to leadership because of their integrity and faithful discharge of work responsibilities. *"Daniel began distinguishing himself . . . because he possessed an extraordinary spirit, and the king planned to appoint him over the entire kingdom . . . inasmuch as he was faithful, and no negligence or corruption was to be found in him"* (Daniel 6:3-4). Your character, honesty, hard work, and excellence in your job earn you the right to share Christ and promulgate biblical values in business.

 SUGGESTED RESOURCES

Teamwork

The Performance Factor—Unlocking the Secrets of Teamwork
by Pat McMillan
Broadman & Holman Publishers

Core Values

Built to Last
by Jim Collins
Harper Business

EXECUTIVE SUMMARY – CHAPTER 6

1. It is important to document the business's core values.

2. Leaders should use teams effectively to accomplish specific business objectives.

3. Scripture clearly discourages partnerships comprised of Christians and those who do not know the Lord.

4. Before going into a partnership, document the agreement in writing.

MARKETING

*"You shall not steal, nor deal falsely,
nor lie to one another."*
Leviticus 19:11

MARKETING HOMEWORK
Homework to be completed for Chapter 7

Before attending class complete the:
☐ Scripture to Memorize
☐ Marketing Homework

 SCRIPTURE TO MEMORIZE

"You shall not steal, nor deal falsely, nor lie to one another" (Leviticus 19:11).

DAY ONE – REVIEW CHAPTER 6

Read the Organization Notes on pages 100-110 and answer.

1. What in the Notes was particularly helpful or challenging?

2. How will you apply what you learned to your personal and business life?

112

MARKETING HOMEWORK

Read Leviticus 19:11. *"You shall not steal, nor deal falsely, nor lie to one another."*

And read 1 Peter 1:15-16. *"Be holy yourselves also in all your behavior; because it is written, 'You shall be holy, for I am holy.'"*

1. What do these verses communicate to you about God's demand for honesty?

    Leviticus 19:11 —

    1 Peter 1:15-16 —

Read Proverbs 26:28. *"A lying tongue hates those it crushes."*

And read Romans 13:9-10. *"If you love your neighbor as much as you love yourself you will not want to harm or cheat him, or kill him or steal from him. . . . Love does no wrong to anyone"* (TLB).

2. According to these passages, can you practice dishonesty and still love your neighbor? Why or why not?

3. Are you consistently honest in even the smallest details of your business, especially in marketing and sales? If not, what will you do to change?

DAY THREE – MARKETING AND SALES

1. Describe the basic marketing and sales practices of your business that have been the most successful.

2. How is integrity in marketing and sales most often compromised in your industry?

3. In what ways are you most tempted to compromise in your marketing and sales?

DAY FOUR – PRICING AND DISCOUNTS

Read Deuteronomy 25:13, 15-16. *"Do not have two differing weights in your bag—one heavy, one light. . . . You must have accurate and honest measures. . . . For the Lord your God detests anyone who does these things, anyone who deals dishonestly"* (NIV).

And read Proverbs 11:1. *"A false balance is an abomination to the Lord, but a just weight is His delight."*

1. What do these verses say about pricing your products or services honestly?

   Deuteronomy 25:13, 15-16 —

   Proverbs 11:1 —

MARKETING HOMEWORK

2. Describe your pricing and discount policy.

3. Describe any changes in your pricing or discounting that you need to make to please the Lord.

DAY FIVE – RESTITUTION AND BRIBES

Read Leviticus 6:4-5. *"Then it shall be, when he sins and becomes guilty, that he shall restore what he took by robbery . . . or anything about which he swore falsely; he shall make restitution for it in full, and add to it one-fifth more. He shall give it to the one to whom it belongs."*

And read Luke 19:8. *"If I have defrauded anyone of anything, I will give back four times as much."*

1. What does the Bible say about restitution?

2. If you have acquired anything dishonestly, how will you make restitution?

Read Exodus 23:8. *"Do not accept a bribe, for a bribe blinds those who see and twists the words of the righteous"* (NIV).

And read Proverbs 15:27. *"A greedy man brings trouble to his family, but he who hates bribes will live"* (NIV).

3. What does the Bible say about bribes?

4. Have you ever been asked to give or take a bribe? If so, describe what happened.

DAY SIX – CASE STUDY AND PRACTICAL APPLICATION

Note: You may read the Marketing Notes prior to completing this Day Six Homework if you wish.

CASE STUDY

For 10 years Michelle Dixon has owned a residential mortgage brokerage that specializes in house loans for those with poor credit ratings. Her office serves a growing community where about 40 percent of the population are relatively recent immigrants to the United States. Their newness to the culture means they are not educated borrowers.

A number of new competitors have entered into the market within the past two years. They market aggressively and do not disclose accurately the interest rate and fees that will be charged.

Michelle's business is off more than 50 percent even though the housing market for her clients is strong. She worries that the business will not survive. She is considering changing her marketing strategy from one of honest disclosure to one that is similar to her new competition.

Analysis

1. Define the problem/issue.

2. Identify the people involved.

3. Identify special circumstances and potential consequences.

4. What actions do you think should be taken? Why?

5. How would God be honored and glorified by these actions?

Application

Based on this case study and what you have learned from the Marketing lesson, please answer the following questions.

1. What insight have you gained concerning your business?

2. What changes might you need to make in the operation of your business?

3. What results would you hope to see?

PRACTICAL APPLICATION

Analyze your existing marketing policies and practices. Describe what changes, if any, you need to make.

MARKETING NOTES ♛

Please complete the Marketing Homework (Days 1-5) before reading these notes.

A wide variety of marketing methods exist today: television, radio, newspaper, the Web, direct mail, telephone sales, conventions, personal sales calls, referrals, etc. Depending upon your business and budget, you may choose to employ a number of these marketing techniques. Regardless of your marketing method, however, the best long-term strategy is to confine your marketing promises to the simple truth and then deliver what you promised.

In any business, a satisfied customer who returns and becomes a source of word-of-mouth referrals is the least expensive, most effective way to market. Unfortunately, honesty in sales and marketing is easily compromised. Have you ever been tempted not to tell a customer the *whole* truth when you are trying to sell something? Have you ever been tempted not to pay all taxes legally due the government? These decisions are especially difficult because everyone around us seems to be acting dishonestly—particularly in the area of sales and marketing.

The ethical standards of marketing are often well defined by law, which you can think of as the bottom floor of standards. A second level of standards may be an association code of ethics for your particular profession. A third level of standards is the company's policy and values. Then there are God's principles of honesty and integrity.

James Cash Penney was one of the nation's great retailing pioneers. Born the son of a minister in 1875, he went into the dry-goods business as a salesman. He quickly became a store manager and part owner of his own store.

Penney was committed to conducting business by biblical principles. He insisted on selling only quality merchandise, keeping price markups to a minimum and operating by the Golden Rule.

By 1928, his business had grown to a chain of more than a thousand J. C. Penney stores. In describing the secret of his success, Penney said, "There are no secrets. In retailing, the formula is a basic liking for human beings, plus integrity and hard work."[1]

Any sales or marketing professional will tell you how important it is to maintain a good reputation. Unfortunately, some Christians have earned a poor one. How many times have you heard people criticize the unethical practices of a Christian?

In this chapter we will survey what Scripture says about honesty and how it applies to marketing, sales, and pricing.

Hundreds of verses in the Bible communicate the Lord's desire for us to be completely honest. For instance, Proverbs 20:23 reads, *"The Lord loathes all cheating and dishonesty"* (TLB). And Proverbs 12:22 states, *"Lying lips are an abomination to the Lord."* From Proverbs 6:16-17 we read, *"The Lord hates . . . a lying tongue."*

The God of truth
Truthfulness is one of God's attributes. He is repeatedly identified as the God of truth. *"I am . . . the truth"* (John 14:6). He commands us to reflect His honest and holy character: *"Be holy yourselves also in all your behavior; because it is written, 'You shall be holy, for I am holy'"* (1 Peter 1:15-16).

WHY BE HONEST?
When being dishonest, we are acting as if the living God doesn't even exist! We believe that God is not able to provide exactly what we need even though He has promised to do so (Matthew 6:33). We decide to take matters into our own hands and handle them in our own dishonest way. We are also acting as if God is incapable of discovering our dishonesty and is powerless to discipline us. If we really believe God will discipline us, then we will not consider acting dishonestly.

Honest behavior is an issue of faith. An honest decision may look foolish in light of what we can see, but the godly person knows that Jesus Christ is alive even though He is invisible. Every honest decision strengthens our faith in the living God and helps us grow into a closer relationship with Christ. However, if we choose to be dishonest, we essentially deny our Lord and violate the first and greatest commandment. It is impossible to love God with all our heart, soul and mind if, at the same time, we are dishonest and act as if He does not exist.

Here is another practical reason for guarding our integrity: Our heavenly Father ultimately will not allow us to keep anything we have acquired dishonestly. Proverbs 13:11 reads, *"Wealth obtained by fraud dwindles."* Think about this for a moment: If you are a parent and one of your children steals something, do you allow the child to keep it? Of course not. You require its return because the child's character would be destroyed if he or she kept stolen property. Not only do you insist on its return, you usually want the child to experience enough discomfort to produce a lasting impression. For instance, you might have the child confess the theft and ask forgiveness from the store manager. When our heavenly Father lovingly disciplines us, He usually does it in such a way that we will not forget. This can be painful or embarrassing.

We cannot practice dishonesty and love our neighbor.
Dishonest behavior also violates the second commandment, *"You shall love your neighbor as yourself"* (Mark 12:31). Romans 13:9-10 reads, *"If you love your neighbor as much as you love yourself you will not want to harm or cheat him, or kill him or steal from him . . . love does no wrong to anyone"* (TLB).

We must understand that when we act dishonestly, we are stealing from

MARKETING NOTES

another person. We may rationalize that it is only a corporation or the government suffering the loss, but the bottom line confirms that it is the customers, business owners or other taxpayers from whom we are stealing. It is just as if we took the money from their wallets. Dishonesty always injures people; the victim is always a person.

Credibility for evangelism

Another reason our Lord demands absolute honesty in the way we handle money is to demonstrate the reality of Jesus Christ to those who do not yet know Him.

Sean told his neighbor, Jim, how he could come to know Christ as his personal Savior. Jim snarled, "Well, I know a businessman who goes to church and talks a lot about Jesus, but watch out if you ever get in a business deal with him! He'd cheat his own grandmother! If that's what it means to be a Christian, I don't want any part of it!"

Our actions speak louder than our words. Scripture says to *"Prove yourselves to be blameless and innocent, children of God above reproach in the midst of a crooked and perverse generation, among whom you appear as lights in the world"* (Philippians 2:15).

Our honesty can influence people for Jesus Christ.

Robert Adams was in the used manufacturing-equipment business and had been trying to sell a very expensive specialized piece of equipment. Cash flow was extremely tight. Finally, an interested buyer decided to purchase it but at the last moment said, "I'll buy it, but only on one condition—you don't report the full sale price so I won't have to pay all the sales tax."

Although he was tempted to comply with the demand, Robert responded, "I'm sorry, I can't do that because Jesus Christ is my Lord." Robert later said, "You should have witnessed the buyer's reaction. He almost went into shock! Then an interesting thing happened; his attitude completely changed. Not only did he purchase the equipment, but rarely have I seen anyone as open to the truth about knowing Jesus Christ in a personal way."

Because Robert acted honestly even though it was going to cost him money (*"Prove yourselves to be blameless and innocent, children of God above reproach"*), he demonstrated to this person (*"a crooked and perverse generation"*) the reality of a personal faith in Jesus Christ (*"appear as lights in the world"*).

HONESTY OF LEADERS

The Lord is especially concerned with the honesty of leaders because they influence their subordinates.

The owner of a trucking business began wearing cowboy boots to work. Within six months, all the men in his office were in boots. He suddenly changed to a traditional business shoe and six months later all the men were wearing business shoes.

In a similar way, a dishonest leader produces dishonest followers. *"If a ruler pays attention to falsehood, all his ministers become wicked"* (Proverbs 29:12).

Leaders in business must set the example of honesty before they can expect those under their authority to do the same.

The president of a large international construction company was asked why her company did not work in countries where bribes are a way of life. She responded, "We never build in those countries, no matter how profitable the project may appear, because we can't afford to. If our employees know we are acting dishonestly, they will eventually become thieves. Their dishonesty will ultimately cost us more than we could ever earn on a project."

During an effort to reduce expenses, a company discovered that employees frequently made personal long-distance telephone calls at the office and charged them to the company. The company president had unwittingly fueled this problem. He had reasoned that because he placed approximately the same number of company long-distance calls on his home phone as personal long-distance calls on the company phone, a detailed accounting and reimbursement were unnecessary.

But his employees knew only of his calls at work. They concluded that if this dishonest practice was acceptable for the boss, it was acceptable for all. Leaders should *"abstain from all appearance of evil"* (1 Thessalonians 5:22, KJV), because their actions influence others.

INTEGRITY IN SALES AND MARKETING

When people feel cheated in business, it is often because of expectations that were subtly implied. People tend to hear what they want to hear, and some salespeople are happy to let them do so if it serves their purpose.

Ask yourself these questions:

- Does your advertising make suggestions or raise expectations that you cannot completely fulfill?
- Are your customers going to discover something later that they will wish you had told them up front?
- How do you feel about having to explain to a customer what the ad or the sales agreement *really* meant?
- Does your contract or estimate contain provisions that customers will never know about unless they read the fine print or ask the right questions? Does the wording obscure the true meaning?
- Do you "oversell" by promising or implying that your product or service will do more than it really will?
- When selling or marketing, do you ever deceive customers by subtly leading them to believe something that is not true?

As a Christian, it's not enough to simply tell the truth when someone knows to ask the right questions. You want to be straightforward with people in such a way that you don't allow them to harbor false expectations about your product, its delivery, service or price. Some call it full disclosure or telling "the truth and nothing but the truth." That approach will affect every aspect of the marketing process from design to customer service. Using biblical terminology, it is doing unto others as you would have them do unto you. You can personalize that verse and ask yourself, *Am I dealing as straightforwardly with my clients or customers as I would like for them to deal with me?*

WHAT TO DO WHEN DISHONEST

What do we need to do if we have sold or acquired anything dishonestly? The Bible is clear: We must make restitution. *"Then it shall be, when he sins and becomes guilty, that he shall restore what he took by robbery . . . or anything about which he swore falsely; he shall make restitution for it in full, and add to it one-fifth more. He shall give it to the one to whom it belongs"* (Leviticus 6:4-5).

Restitution is a tangible expression of repentance and an effort to correct a wrong. Zaccheus is a good example of fulfilling this principle. He promised Jesus, *"If I have defrauded anyone of anything, I will give back four times as much"* (Luke 19:8).

DISCOUNTING DECISIONS

"I'm sorry, ma'am, but I can't cut the price on that car any more," Kris Burgess whined. "As you can see from the dealer invoice, we're at rock bottom. Check with any other dealer in town and you'll see we're always the lowest. I'll only make a hundred dollars on the sale, and that's hardly enough to keep the doors open."

"I wouldn't want you to lose any money," Elizabeth Evans responded. "I know you have to make a living too. I guess I'll take it. If you're only making a hundred dollars, surely no one else could beat your price."

"That's for sure, ma'am," Kris replied.

Standing outside the sales manager's doorway, Chuck Crouse, the general manager, chuckled beneath his breath, "Boy, Kris is a sharp salesperson. He could talk a dog out of his fleas."

Chuck knew that the invoice Kris had shown Elizabeth was only partially accurate. The invoice amount *was* what the agency was billed, but with dealer incentives and service charges, the sale would net hundreds of dollars more for the company. Chuck was pleased that he had what it took to make his dealership successful.

Soon after Elizabeth signed her contract, the local county commissioner, Marvin Terrell, came into the dealership. "Chuck, I need to buy a new car, but I want your best deal. I don't want any of that dealer-cost stuff, Chuck. I don't mind you making a hundred or so, but I don't want to pay for your kid's college education."

"Marv, I'll guarantee you a thousand less than Mrs. Evans just paid for the same car."

That is what a Christian salesman overheard at the agency he had just gone to work for as he sat in his office studying the sales literature. He had taken the job because the owner was a leader in his church.

Proverbs 11:1 reads, *"A false balance is an abomination to the Lord, but a just weight is His delight."* Unfortunately, Chuck Crouse uses a false balance, one that has differing weights for different customers.

WHAT PRICE DIFFERENCES ARE LEGITIMATE?
There are ethical reasons why a merchant might charge one person more or less than another.

1. Volume discounts
Many businesses offer discounts based on quantity. This is an honest and acceptable practice, provided everyone has the same opportunity to receive the discount. If you purchase an item at one price and then later learn that someone else bought 50 of the items for a lower average cost, you shouldn't feel cheated, particularly if the salesperson explained that you could get the same discount. There was no intent to deceive and, therefore, no differing weight.

2. Cash discounts
Many merchants offer discounts to customers who pay in cash. This same offer is often extended to payments made within a certain time, such as 10 days from the date of billing. As long as this offer is extended to all customers, there is no ethical problem.

3. Class discounts
Discounts are offered to senior citizens, college students, the unemployed and so on. This policy it is not the equivalent of a differing weight as long as it is clearly posted and available to anyone within the class.

A FAIR PRICE STANDARD
Wouldn't it be great to be able to buy something, knowing that you received as fair a price as possible? That if the salesperson said, "That's as low as we can go and make a profit," you could believe it? That should be the norm for a Christian's business.

Harry and Mark manufactured equipment used by companies to test their own electronic products. They built good equipment that, unfortunately, didn't sell well, and the company was in financial difficulty.

They met Nathan Shadburn, a potential buyer of several million dollars' worth of their equipment. He wanted to use their design to build test equipment for the government.

"But there's one thing," he said as he finished his presentation. "We'll have to raise the price of the equipment from $8,000 to $40,000 a unit."

"Why?" Harry asked. "Our costs won't be any more for the government model."

"Well, the government always pays more for what it buys. I mean, it's practically un-American not to charge the government at least four times more. Your equipment won't be considered any good if it doesn't cost at least $30,000."

"It's not right to charge the government more than we would any other customer unless there are higher costs involved," Harry said.

"There will be some additional costs associated with selling to the government, but basically it's whatever the traffic will bear," Shadburn said with a wink.

"Well, I won't do it," Harry said. "I believe that you charge a fair price for a good product, and people will appreciate it."

"Come on, Harry," his partner said. "If the government wants to pay more, let them."

"It's a matter of honesty," Harry replied. "As long as I own half of this company, we'll stick with the policies the Bible teaches. It doesn't matter whether other people know we cheated; the Lord will know."

"If you aren't willing to let me mark the equipment up, I don't want to handle it," Shadburn said as a challenge.

With that, Harry got up to leave. "We don't have anything else to talk about, then."

Shadburn was flabbergasted. "Wait a minute. You don't mean you're going to walk out on this deal! I know you need the business. I can use $20 million of your equipment over the next few years."

"I'm sorry," Harry said, "My beliefs are worth more than $20 million. We'll be glad to do business, Mr. Shadburn, but not at unfair prices."

Over the next few weeks, Shadburn talked with Harry several times, but Harry turned down every offer. "Mr. Shadburn, you need to realize that I am not negotiating for a better deal. As a Christian, I must follow the principles of God's Word, one of which is charging each customer fairly. I can't mark it up just because the government is the buyer."

A month later, Mr. Shadburn called and said, "I was skeptical the last time I was here. I thought you were just trying to hold out for more money. Now I realize that you're really serious about being honest. I'm getting too calloused by working around so many dishonest people. I apologize, and I still would like to handle your equipment—at the standard price. I know you are having cash-flow problems, which makes your decision not to allow me to sell a marked-up version even more impressive. I'm willing to prepay the first $500,000 worth of equipment for delivery to the government. I'd also like to invest in your company. It's not often I meet honest men, and I believe what you said about God blessing you. I'd like to be in on that."

Nathan Shadburn ultimately invested over $2 million in the business. Two years after the first meeting, Harry prayed with Nathan to receive Christ. He became their most active board member and helped to arrange several large sales that built the company into a multimillion-dollar-a-year business. *"Much wealth is in the house of the righteous, but trouble is in the income of the wicked"* (Proverbs 15:6).

COMMITMENT TO TOTAL HONESTY

God requires us to be totally honest because even the smallest act of dishonesty is sin. And even the smallest sin interrupts our fellowship with the Lord. The smallest "white lie" will harden our hearts, making our consciences increasingly insensitive to sin and deafening our ears to the still, small voice of the Lord. This single cancer cell of small dishonesty multiplies and spreads to greater dishonesty. *"Whoever is dishonest with very little will also be dishonest with much"* (Luke 16:10, NIV).

An event in Abraham's life is an illustration of faithfulness in small matters. In Genesis 14, the king of Sodom offered Abraham to keep all the goods Abraham had recovered when he returned from successfully rescuing the people of Sodom. But Abraham answered, *"I have sworn to the Lord God Most High, possessor of heaven and earth, that I will not take a thread or a sandal thong or anything that is yours"* (Genesis 14:22-23).

Just as Abraham was unwilling to take so much as a thread or a sandal thong, we challenge you to make a similar commitment in this area of honesty. Make a covenant not to be dishonest in your marketing or sales or any other part of your business. It could be stated as simply as this: **Regardless of the consequences, I commit to always obey the Lord and do the right thing.** Living out this commitment will not be easy, but remembering these principles will assist you:

- God is more interested in developing my character than my comfort.
- I will face challenging circumstances in which my commitment to honesty will be tested.
- God is the One who ultimately provides for and prospers us. My responsibility is to conduct my business faithfully in ways that please the Lord, trusting Him for provision.

The people of God must be honest in every business matter. May the Lord strengthen and encourage you as you seek to do just that.

---

[1] From Portrait by Charles Cross, AHC Collections

EXECUTIVE SUMMARY – CHAPTER 7

1. The Lord requires that we be totally honest.

2. Leaders are commanded to be honest because they influence their subordinates for good or evil.

3. We should market and sell with complete integrity.

4. We must be careful to price and discount fairly.

PLANNING

CONTENTS

"The plans of the diligent lead to profit as surely as haste leads to poverty."

Proverbs 21:5, NIV

Before attending class complete the:
☐ Scripture to Memorize
☐ Planning Homework

 SCRIPTURE TO MEMORIZE

"The plans of the diligent lead to profit as surely as haste leads to poverty"
(Proverbs 21:5, NIV).

DAY ONE – REVIEW CHAPTER 7

Read the Marketing Notes on pages 118-125 and answer.

1. What in the Notes was particularly helpful or challenging?

2. How will you apply what you learned to your personal and business life?

Read Proverbs 21:5. *"The plans of the diligent lead to profit as surely as haste leads to poverty."*

1. What does this verse say about the benefits of planning and the consequences of not planning?

2. Describe your experience with business planning. What results have you seen?

Read Luke 14:28-30. *"For which one of you, when he wants to build a tower, does not first sit down and calculate the cost, to see if he has enough to complete it? Otherwise, when he has laid a foundation and is not able to finish, all who observe it begin to ridicule him, saying, 'This man began to build and was not able to finish.'"*

3. How does the Lord view planning according to this illustration?

Read Psalm 20:4. *"May he [the Lord] give you the desire of your heart and make all your plans succeed"* (NIV).

And read Proverbs 16:9. *"Man plans his way, but the Lord directs his steps."*

4. According to these passages, what part does God play in your plans?

Read the Planning Notes on pages 133 to 146.

1. Make a brief list of the items from the Notes that were particularly helpful or challenging.

2. How will you apply each of these to your personal and business life?

DAY FOUR — PERSONAL PLAN

Draft a plan to practice the disciplines that will help you develop your character and grow closer to Christ. Share your plan with your group. Here are several suggestions.

1. Avoid a plan that is too ambitious to implement immediately.
2. Select a person to hold you accountable to the plan. Decide how often you will meet.
3. If you are married, discuss the following disciplines with your spouse. It is much easier to practice the disciplines if your spouse encourages you or participates.

MY SPIRITUAL DISCIPLINES PLAN:

1. Bible Reading and Study

How often—

How much time, when, and where—

Select the Bible or Bible study program—

2. Prayer

How often—

How much time, when, and where—

List people and things for which to pray—

3. **Time alone with God**

How often—

How much time—

Location—

4. **Fellowship with other Christians**

How I can become involved in a local church—

Type of small group I will participate in—

Location and frequency of group meetings—

5. **Reading Christian books**

How often—

How much time, when, and where—

Books I will read—

DAY FIVE – BUSINESS MISSION STATEMENT AND BUSINESS PLAN

A Mission Statement is a very important tool. It helps the organization remain focused and reject opportunities and activities that are not consistent with its mission. It should be clear, concise, and short enough to memorize easily. It answers the question, "Why does this business exist?"

DEVELOP YOUR MISSION STATEMENT AND SHARE IT WITH YOUR GROUP.

Follow these steps for developing your Mission Statement:

1. Pray.
2. Answer these:

   ■ The product or service is—

   ■ The product or service is used by—

■ The purpose of the business is to—

■ God's purpose in the business is met by—

■ We are fulfilling God's purpose in our business when—

3. Discuss the answers with your leadership team and draft several Mission Statements.
4. Put the drafts aside for two weeks, then meet with your leadership team to edit and select the Mission Statement.
5. Review after six months and modify as necessary.

DEVELOP YOUR BUSINESS PLAN. (SEE PAGES 142-144 FOR A BUSINESS PLAN OUTLINE.)

DESCRIBE YOUR PLAN FOR ACCOUNTABILITY TO EXECUTE THE BUSINESS PLAN.

DAY SIX – THE ENTIRE STUDY

1. What has been the most helpful part of this entire study for you?

2. Are you going to become part of a continuing small group? If so, describe how you plan to do so.

PLANNING NOTES

Please complete the Planning Homework (Days 1-2) before reading these notes.

THE BIBLE ON PLANNING

The Lord encourages us to plan. Proverbs 21:5 says, *"The plans of the diligent lead to profit as surely as haste leads to poverty"* (NIV). Jesus gave this illustration: *"For which of you, when he wants to build a tower, does not first sit down and calculate the cost, to see if he has enough to complete it? Otherwise, when he has laid a foundation and is not able to finish, all who observe it begin to ridicule him, saying, 'This man began to build and was not able to finish'"* (Luke 14:28-30).

The Lord Himself planned and created a superbly ordered universe. *"God is not a God of disorder"* (1 Corinthians 14:33, NIV).

GOD'S CONTROL OF OUR PLANS

We are to plan, but we must recognize that the Lord has ultimate control over the outcome. Proverbs 16:9 reads, *"The mind of man plans his way, but the Lord directs his steps."*

And Proverbs 19:21 tells us, *"Many are the plans in a man's heart, but it is the Lord's purpose that prevails"* (NIV). Someone said it this way, "Make your plan, but write it in pencil and give God the eraser. Only He really knows what's best."

PERSONAL PLANNING

If leaders are not growing in their personal relationship with Christ, the culture of the business will ultimately reflect that fact. This will hinder the implementation of strategies based on biblical principles and values. For any business to glorify Christ, the leaders' spiritual lives must be healthy. That is why business people should first develop their Personal Plan.

The first step in developing your plan is to make sure that you have a personal relationship with the Lord. Five biblical truths explain how you can enter into this relationship.

1. God loves you and wants you to know Him and experience a meaningful life.

God created people in His own image, and He desires an intimate relationship with each of us. *"For God so loved the world, that He gave His only begotten Son, that whoever believes in Him shall not perish, but have eternal life"* (John 3:16). *"I [Jesus] came that they may have life, and have it abundantly"* (John 10:10).

God the Father loves you. He gave His only Son, Jesus Christ, to die for you. Perhaps this example will help you understand His love.

PLANNING NOTES

In the 1992 Olympics in Barcelona, Spain, a British runner named Derek Redmond was ready for his moment in the sun. He had trained relentlessly for this lifelong dream of winning the gold medal in the 400-meter race. As the gun sounded for the semifinals, Derek knew that everything hinged on the next minute.

Then, tragically, as he entered the backstretch, Redmond felt pain in the back of his right leg. A torn hamstring sent him sprawling on the surface of the track.

Instinctively, Derek struggled to his feet in excruciating pain and began hopping on one leg toward the finish line. Suddenly, a large man came bounding from the stands. Flinging aside security guards, he made his way onto the field and threw his arms around Derek. It was Jim Redmond, Derek's father.

"Son, you don't have to do this," he said.

"Yes, Dad, I do," Derek assured him.

"All right then, let's finish this together," said the older man. And that's exactly what they did. With the son's head frequently buried in his father's shoulder, they made it to the end of the race as the crowd rose to their feet, weeping and cheering!

Derek Redmond did not win the gold medal in the Olympics, but he won something far more valuable. He walked away from the race with the memory of a father who not only cheered in the stands but also loved him too much to watch him suffer from a distance—a father who came down out of the stands and entered the race with him, staying beside him every step of the way.

Our heavenly Father watches us with eyes of love and affection. He cares for us too deeply to stay in heaven, looking down on us, watching us fall and fail. Instead, He came down out of the stands and into our race in the person of His precious Son, Jesus Christ.[1]

2. Unfortunately, we are separated from God.

God is holy—which means God is perfect—and He cannot have a relationship with anyone who is not also perfect. Every person has sinned, and the consequence of sin is separation from God. *"All have sinned and fall short of the glory of God" (Romans 3:23)*. *"Your sins have cut you off from God"* (Isaiah 59:2, TLB).

The diagram below illustrates an enormous gap that separates people from God. Individuals try without success to bridge this gap through their own efforts, such as philosophy, religion, material goods, charitable activity or living a good moral life.

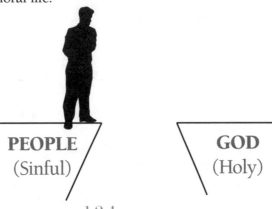

PEOPLE
(Sinful)

GOD
(Holy)

3. God's only provision to bridge this gap is Jesus Christ.

Jesus Christ died on the cross to pay the penalty for our sin. The next diagram illustrates how Jesus bridged the gap from man to God. *"Jesus said to him, 'I am the way, and the truth, and the life; no one comes to the Father but through Me'"* (John 14:6). *"God demonstrates His own love toward us, in that while we were yet sinners, Christ died for us"* (Romans 5:8).

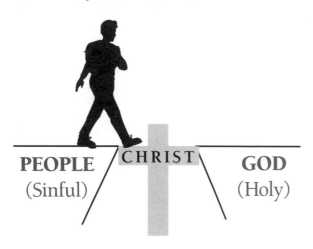

PEOPLE /CHRIST\   **GOD**
(Sinful)   (Holy)

4. This relationship is a gift from God.

By an act of faith, you can receive the free gift of a relationship with God. *"By grace you have been saved through faith; and that not of yourselves, it is the gift of God; not as a result of works"* (Ephesians 2:8-9).

5. We must each receive Jesus Christ individually.

We have only to ask Jesus Christ to come into our life and become our Savior and Lord. A relationship with the living God is available to you through Jesus Christ. Nothing in life compares with the privilege of knowing Christ personally.

If you desire to know the Lord and are not certain whether you have this relationship, we encourage you to receive Christ right now. Pray a prayer similar to this suggested one: "Father God, I need you. I invite Jesus to come into my life as my Savior and Lord and to make me the person you want me to be. Thank you for forgiving my sins and giving me the gift of eternal life."

You could fulfill every principle for becoming a faithful manager of your business, but without a relationship with Christ, your efforts will be in vain. If you ask Christ into your life, please tell your small group leaders so they will be able to assist you in your spiritual growth.

Once you have confirmed that you know Jesus Christ as your Savior, the next step is to understand that God plays a role and we play a part in the maturing of our character. This is important because when people develop godly character, it gives the Lord more freedom to use them in their business in eternally significant ways.

Author Richard Foster said, "To think rightly about God is, in an important sense, to have everything right. To think wrongly about God is, in an important sense, to have everything wrong." A. W. Tozer wrote, "Nothing twists and deforms the soul more than a low or unworthy conception of God."

First, you need to recognize how deeply and extravagantly God loves you, and the part He plays in developing your character.

GOD LOVES YOU.
Carefully answer these questions to help you assess your relationship with the Lord.

- Would you like to see your relationship with God as time spent with your very best friend, who rejoices when He hears your voice?
- When you're with Him, do you feel welcomed and valued and totally loved? Or are your times with Him awkward and tense?
- Are you able to be honest and vulnerable with God? Or is He someone with whom you're always trying to act better than you are because you fear that your real self might not be good enough?

In Mark 14:36, Jesus used an intimate name to speak with His heavenly Father: *"Abba."* Abba was the affectionate name a Hebrew child would use for a beloved parent, just as a child in our culture might say "Daddy." We who know Christ may also have this intimacy with the Father. *"God has sent forth the Spirit of His Son into our hearts, crying, 'Abba! Father!'"* (Galatians 4:6).

Learning to think of God as a loving Father comes easier for some than others. Many of us relate to God as we did to earthly fathers. Our ability to trust and be close to God is often determined by the amount of trust and intimacy we experienced with our earthly dad. If our earthly fathers were frequently absent, if they were negligent, abusive or emotionally distant, it is much harder for us to believe that God wants intimacy with us.

God knows what kind of childhood each of us had. He longs to heal any misconception of what a father should be so we can know Him as He is. Unlike our earthly parents who were limited in their ability to love, God is unlimited.[2]

In John 15:9, Jesus makes this remarkable statement, *"Just as the Father has loved Me, I have also loved you; abide in My love."* It is impossible to describe how much God the Father loves God the Son, but Jesus tells us that is how much He loves us.

GOD LOVES YOU SO MUCH, HE SENT THE HOLY SPIRIT.
Apart from receiving Jesus Christ as Savior, no more practical issue exists than understanding the role of the Holy Spirit. Yet many people do not understand who He is, what He does, or how to release His power in their lives.

Scripture identifies the Holy Spirit as God. *"The Lord is the Spirit"* (2 Corinthians 3:17). He is the third person of the Trinity: the Father, the Son, and the Holy Spirit. Jesus drew attention to the Holy Spirit's vital role after His departure when He said, *"It is to your advantage that I go away; for if I do not go away, the Helper will not come to you; but if I go, I will send Him to you . . . But when He, the Spirit of truth, comes, He will guide you into all truth"* (John 16:7, 13).

The Lord left this earth and sent the Helper, the Holy Spirit, to indwell those who know Christ so that we can live the Christian life. *"I have been crucified with Christ; and it is no longer I who live, but Christ lives in me; and the life which I now live in the flesh I live by faith in the Son of God, who loved me and delivered Himself up for me"* (Galatians 2:20).

Our responsibility is to totally submit to the Lord. Yield to Him in unconditional surrender. Everything we are and have must be given to Him to use as He desires. We can abandon ourselves to the Lord because of the confidence we have in His love for us as individuals.

Colossians 1:26-27 reads, *"The mystery that has been kept hidden for ages and generations, but is now disclosed . . . which is Christ in you, the hope of glory"* (NIV). This is staggering! Take time to consider this. The Creator of the universe has chosen to live in the heart of each of us who know Him. Christ living His life in and through you is the secret of the Christian life.

OUR PART IN CHARACTER DEVELOPMENT

Think of spiritual disciplines as spiritual exercises. The apostle Paul instructed the younger Timothy to *"Discipline yourself for the purpose of godliness"* (1 Timothy 4:7). This was a command, not a suggestion.

A close walk with Christ is the goal of these disciplines, and when we remember this, they become a delight instead of drudgery. It's crucial to keep the big picture in mind: the reason to practice spiritual disciplines is not to check another item off our "to do" list; it's to grow closer to Christ and maturity of character. Don't allow this to become a stale exercise; that leads only to frustration.

You must develop a Personal Plan to implement these disciplines.

PLAN TO READ, STUDY AND MEDITATE ON THE BIBLE.
No spiritual discipline is more important than spending time in God's Word. Nothing can substitute for it. In the Bible, God tells us about Himself and His ways, how to live in a way that pleases Him, and what is best and most fulfilling for us.

Jesus often asked questions beginning with the words, "Have you not read?" He assumed that those claiming to be the people of God would have read the Word of God. Unfortunately, this is often not the case. A recent survey found that only 18 percent of Christians read the Bible every day, and 23 percent never do.

When Jesus said, *"Man shall not live on bread alone, but on every word that proceeds out of the mouth of God"* (Matthew 4:4), surely He intended for us to read every word. The Bible makes these remarkable claims about itself: *"The word of God is living and active and sharper than any two-edged sword . . . and*

A close walk with Christ is the goal of these disciplines, and when we remember this, they become a delight instead of drudgery.

able to judge the thoughts and intentions of the heart" (Hebrews 4:12). *"All Scripture is God-breathed and is useful for teaching, rebuking, correcting and training in righteousness, so that the man of God may be thoroughly equipped for every good work"* (2 Timothy 3:16-17, NIV). Since the Scripture is living and God-breathed, shouldn't we read and study it?

Here are four suggestions for consistent success in Bible reading.

1. *Plan the time*. Perhaps one of the main reasons Christians never read through the entire Bible is its sheer length. Do you realize that you can read through the Bible in a year's time by spending only 15 minutes a day? Discipline yourself to find the time. Try to make it the same time every day.

2. *Use a Bible-reading plan.* It's no wonder that those who simply open the Bible at random each day soon drop the discipline. There are effective Bible-reading plans available at Christian bookstores, and many Bibles are designed to read through in a year. One of the best is *The Daily Walk Bible.*

3. *Meditate on one verse each week.* This will change your life. The Lord commanded Joshua, *"This book of the law shall not depart from your mouth, but you shall mediate on it day and night, so that you may be careful to do according to all that is written in it; for then . . . you will have success"* (Joshua 1:8). You may be thinking, "That's great for Joshua, but I've got a company or a household to run! I can't think about the Bible all day long. This sounds good, but it just isn't practical."

   Meditation is the most practical thing in the world. Joshua had two million people to manage, and he was as busy, if not busier, than you are. So how does a busy person meditate on the Bible? Read through a portion of the Bible, and when a verse jumps out at you, write it down. Take it with you, review it, and think about it during the day.

4. *Find a Bible study.* Most of us will be more consistent if we stay involved in a Bible study like this one. We need the structure, encouragement and accountability of a group. One of the greatest benefits of a group is the development of close relationships with others who are seeking to know the Lord better. We strongly recommend the Crown Financial Ministries small group financial study. Visit **Crown.org** to learn more about this outstanding study.

PLAN TO PRAY.

If prayer could be unnecessary for anyone, surely it would have been for Jesus Christ, the sinless Son of God. However, it was one of the dominant habits of His life and a frequent theme in His teaching. Even in the midst of His busy public ministry, the Lord consistently spent time alone with His Heavenly Father. *"Jesus often withdrew to lonely places and prayed"* (Luke 5:16, NIV).

Throughout history, spiritual leaders have recognized the importance of prayer. Samuel Chadwick said, "The one concern of the devil is to keep Christians from praying. He fears nothing from our prayerless work, prayerless religion. He laughs at our toil, he mocks our wisdom, but he trembles when we pray." And it was John Wesley's conviction that "God does nothing but in answer to prayer."

One of the most important prerequisites to true intimacy with the Lord is honesty in our prayer lives. Don't over-spiritualize your thoughts and feelings. If you are hurting, say so. If you are confused, seek His guidance. If your joy is bubbling over, let it bubble over in praise.

Most of us will be more consistent if we establish a regular time in our daily schedule to pray. It is also helpful to develop a list of people and circumstances for which to pray.

PLAN TO HAVE TIME ALONE WITH GOD.

The hurried life is the norm in our culture. Family, business, social, community, and church commitments dominate our time. The average person also spends hours each day watching television, surfing the Internet or participating in some form of entertainment.

Analyze how you are spending your time. Perhaps modifying your commitments or rescheduling your priorities would allow you to invest more time in getting to know Christ better. It would enable you to be quiet before Him and listen for His voice.

God told Elijah, "'Stand on the mountain in the presence of the Lord, for the Lord is about to pass by.' Then a great and powerful wind tore the mountains apart and shattered the rocks before the Lord, but the Lord was not in the wind. After the wind there was an earthquake, but the Lord was not in the earthquake. After the earthquake came a fire, but the Lord was not in the fire. And after the fire came a gentle whisper. . . . Then a voice said . . . " (1 Kings 19:11-13, NIV). We must be quiet if we are going to hear God's still, small voice.

We suggest that you try something that many today would consider radical. Take a day every quarter to be alone with the Lord. Go to a place that has no television, Internet connection, phone, or other distractions. Take just your Bible, a pen, and some paper. Read. Pray. Rest. Have a really good conversation with the Lord, and write down what you sense He is saying to you.

PLAN TO HAVE FELLOWSHIP WITH OTHER CHRISTIANS.

The Christian life is not one of independence from other Christians but of interdependence with them.

It is important to be part of a church family. Hebrews 10:24-25 reads, "Let us consider how to stimulate one another to love and good deeds, not forsaking our own assembling together, as is the habit of some, but encouraging one another; and all the more as you see the day drawing near."

We recommend that you meet regularly with a group of business peers to share your lives with one another. Experience the benefits and safety of having a group of people who love each other and give wise counsel even when it hurts. "Iron sharpens iron, so one man sharpens another" (Proverb 27:17).

Visit **Crown.org/Business** for recommendations on outstanding business ministries that specialize in fellowship and biblical teaching for businesspeople.

PLAN TO READ CHRISTIAN BOOKS.

The person who desires to grow spiritually should read consistently. The doctor who wants to serve his patients well must read to keep abreast of important medical progress. Unfortunately, the habit of reading solid Christian literature is rare.

Because there are so many books available today, it is important to be selective in what you read. We can afford to read only the best, the ones that will be most helpful to us.

1. **Plan how to read.** Reading should involve not only scanning the words but also meditating on the thoughts they express. Charles H. Spurgeon counseled his students: "Master the books you have. Read them thoroughly. Read and reread them. Let them go into your very self. Peruse a good book several times and make notes and analyses of it. A student will find that his mental constitution is more affected by one book thoroughly mastered than by twenty books merely skimmed."

2. **Plan what to read.** The positive power of even one book is impossible to estimate. The following Christian books have profoundly impacted their readers.

> *Humility,* Andrew Murray, Moody Press, Chicago, IL
> *The Pursuit of God,* A.W. Tozer, Christian Publications, Harrisburg, PA
> *Man in the Mirror,* Patrick Morley, Zondervan Publishing House, Grand Rapids, MI
> *Ordering Your Private World,* Gordon MacDonald, Oliver-Nelson Books, Nashville, TN
> *Experiencing God Study,* Henry T. Blackaby, LifeWay Press, Nashville, TN
> *Hudson Taylor's Spiritual Secrets,* Howard Taylor, Moody Press, Chicago, IL
> *Half Time,* Bob Buford, Zondervan Publishing House, Grand Rapids, MI
> *Spiritual Leadership,* J. Oswald Sanders, Moody Press, Chicago, IL
> *Business by the Book,* Larry Burkett, Thomas Nelson Publishers, Nashville, TN

Reading good biographies is an important part of a Christian's education. They reveal the importance of godly character, provide illustrations for developing life goals, and teach that sacrifice and self-denial are necessary to fulfill God's purposes. As we read about the lives of great and consecrated men and women, we become more inspired to invest our lives in building God's kingdom.

PERSONAL PLANNING SUMMARY

The basis for developing godly character is understanding that God loves you deeply and lives inside each person who has invited Christ to be his or her Savior. He is the One who ultimately molds character. However, maturity in Christ also depends on our faithfulness in planning and practicing the spiritual disciplines of Bible study, prayer, serving, fellowshipping, and time alone with God.

Unfortunately, 80 percent of all business startups do not survive beyond the second year. Many fail because they do not have an adequate business plan. Without a plan, they attempt to start with inadequate capital for their cash flow needs—funding a growing inventory, accounts receivable, and personnel requirements.

The biblical approach to business planning begins with an acknowledgment of God's role. Proverbs 3:5-6 reads, *"Trust in the Lord with all your heart, and do not lean on your own understanding. In all your ways acknowledge Him, and He will make your paths straight."*

When drawing up a plan for a new or existing business, you should *"in all your ways acknowledge Him"*; that is, recognize God's part in every aspect of your business.

STEPS IN BUSINESS PLANNING

1. Identify the Core Values.

We discussed the importance of establishing the Core Values of the business in Chapter 6.

2. Draft the Mission Statement.

The second step in developing an effective business plan is a clear Mission Statement that defines the reason for the existence of the business. It takes thoughtful work to craft an easy-to-memorize simple sentence or two that clearly reflects the purpose of the business.

A Mission Statement needs to be purpose-oriented, that is, it should flow out of some deeper purpose. For example, you could say that your mission was to make as much money as possible selling used cars. But a more purposeful, value-based Mission Statement would look something like this: "Our mission is to glorify Christ by serving people of modest income by providing reliable transportation at a fair price." Every Mission Statement should be written and revised with an eye on purpose and values.

3. Establish measurable objectives.

The third planning step is to establish measurable objectives. For the used-car business, it might look something like this: "Our objective is to sell 25 cars a month, to achieve a 10 percent profit margin and to keep bad debt under one percent of gross sales." Measurable objectives help create a sense of urgency to accomplish your goals. See the outstanding outline for a business plan developed by Marlin Horst on pages 142-144.

4. Develop the plan.

Fourthly, formulate a plan for achieving your objectives—one that is consistent with your mission and values. The plan addresses issues such as, capitalization, organization, marketing, personnel needs, income and expense projections, distribution—everything you need to know and execute to operate a successful business.

When it comes to planning, gather all the facts you can. Good planning is always based on accurate information, and that takes a lot of work. Though you can never know every single detail about a business venture, do all you can to find out everything you can know for sure.

The brilliant military leader General George S. Patton constantly "preached" to his officers about gathering facts. When reviewing the reasons for his commanders' recommendations, he would frequently ask, "How do you know that?" When given the source of the information, he would continue to press the point; "Well, how do *they* know?"

One of the general's principles was, "Know what you know and know what you don't know. Every plan is based on a mixture of known facts, unknowns, and assumptions. Many assumptions can be turned into facts with a little diligence.[3]

Please visit **Crown.org/Business** for a resource that will help you in your business planning and cash-flow projections.

5. After planning, provide for accountability.

Business people often make the mistake of not designing a system of accountability to help the organization remain focused on implementing the business plan. Throughout Scripture, God is revealed as one who holds people accountable. *"After a long time the master of those servants came and settled accounts with them"* (Matthew 25:19). We should do the same for proper execution of the business plan.

6. After planning, measure!

Measuring progress toward your objectives is crucial to implementing the plan. A key principle in planning is that if you can't measure it, you can't manage it! Measurement tells us how well we are executing the plan. It provides the facts we need to adjust our actions to achieve our goals.

BUSINESS PLAN OUTLINE

Business Status Summary
- New business startup plan: Summary of why a startup is viable.
- Current business plan: Describe the current status of the business and why it is necessary to write a new plan.

Business Basics
- How will the business ownership be structured?
- What is the business? Describe in detail what the business will do.
- What justifies the business? Describe why the business makes sense from a personal and financial perspective.
- Why do you want to be in business and what do you hope to accomplish in business?

- What are your short-term, mid-range and long-term goals for the business?
- What is your business model?

Revenue Plan (Know your numbers!)
- Describe each revenue source.
- What can be expected from each source?
- What are the business revenue basics as you know them?
- How will you know when you are on pace with your Financial Plan?

Capitalization Plan
- What will it cost to position yourself to generate the current, mid- and long-range revenue plan (e.g., buildings, equipment, inventory, etc.)? Create a detailed list with actual or projected costs for each expense category.

Marketing Plan
- Who is your competition?
- What is your competitive advantage?
- What will it cost to develop and grow your market share?
- How will you secure ongoing and growing business?

Human Resource Plan
- What personnel will you need to generate the current, mid- and long-range revenue plan? Budget the wage and overhead cost for each.

Financial Plan
- Startup budget: List where and how you will secure capital to accomplish this startup and its desired growth.
- Project a 5-year Balance Sheet (Assets and Liabilities).
- Project a 5-year Profit and Loss Statement (Income and Expense).
  - Income projections
  - Cost of materials/supplies = cost of goods sold
  - Sales overhead
  - General and administrative costs = overhead
  - Projected margin = profit margin
- How will you manage company earnings?
  - Percentage to retained earnings
  - Percentage to profit sharing
  - Percentage to charitable contributions
  - Percentage to stockholder dividends
- Summarize the Financial Plan.
  - Projected cost of sales
  - Projected operations overhead

- Projected general and administrative overhead
- Projected margins

Personal Business Principles and Policies
- List your personal long-term goals for the business: What do you want to accomplish?
- Explain why you have chosen business over employment.
- List your goals in the following areas:
  - Describe how you see business and your commitment to Christ interacting.
  - Use of money.
  - Use of time.
  - Ethical issues.
    - Paying taxes.
    - Policy making.
    - Use of company property.
    - Confession and restitution.
    - Business standards.
    - Personal standards: What are the standards you would want others to hold you to?
    - How will business affect the interconnection of your faith, family, employees, customers, and mentors?
    - Things to avoid—things you should not do.
    - Things you want to accomplish: What is important?
- Employee practices
  - Hiring
  - Motivation
  - Dismissal
  - Steps to dismissal
  - Aborting dismissal
- Management selection
  - Criteria for managers
- Debt-management principles
  - Short-term debt
  - Long-term debt
  - Debt guidelines: List things you would borrow for and things you would not.
- Credit Principles
  - Develop your business credit terms.
  - How will you handle overdue and collection accounts?
- Establish your policy for suing and being sued.

There is an old cliché: "Information without application leads to frustration." You have a large amount of information to evaluate. Now you must decide what God wants you to do with it.

You cannot do everything at once.

Perhaps the easiest way to frustrate yourself and everyone around you is to try to implement all the material from this study immediately. That would be like trying to live the mature Christian life one day after you are introduced to Christ as your Savior. Growth is a process for all of us.

Begin by focusing on one specific area that you see as the key issue in your business. It may be developing good hiring policies or paying a better wage.

Start with your own life.

Here's great news: Neither uncooperative management nor a lack of available resources can keep you from applying biblical principles to your own life. Decide that you're going to love the people around you, even those you don't naturally like.

Start a devotion time in your business.

Almost any business owner can implement a time for devotions. As long as it is optional, it's legal. Those who wish to continue working during that time should be free to do so. Consider bringing in speakers from outside the company to address "felt need" subjects such as drugs, child rearing, husband-wife communication, or getting out of personal debt. Topics like those touch virtually everyone, and if you select speakers with proven track records in their fields, you'll be helping your employees.

Share Christ.

You may want to start sharing Christ with your employees, vendors and customers. But first be sure that you treat employees with love, pay your vendors on time, and provide a good product and service to your customers. Once you demonstrate that Christ is working in your own life, then consider trying ideas that others have found effective. Not every idea will fit every person or business.

The Edwards Baking Company in Atlanta stamps Bible verses into the aluminum pie pans that hold its delicious products. A businessman met Christ one evening after reading such a pie pan in his kitchen. His wife, who was a Christian, had just died after a long illness. On the day of her passing, she had ordered an Edwards pie and left it in the refrigerator for her husband. Just before she died she told him, "I left a surprise for you in the refrigerator, Honey. Read it carefully."

The verse stamped into the pie pan was Romans 8:28: *"We know that God causes all things to work together for good to those who love God, to those who are called according to His purpose."*

A chemical company in Alabama puts a Bible tract in every box of materials it ships. The president of the company questioned the effectiveness of this practice and instructed his shipping department to stop. Within a month he received dozens of letters asking if the company had been sold. Several people told how the tracts had been used to lead fellow employees to the Lord, saying what a testimony it was that a successful businessman would take such a stand for the Lord.

Mark, a personal-injury attorney, has had a significant impact on many of his peers because he has focused on developing close friendships with lawyers on the opposing side. After a case is decided, he routinely invites the attorney out for a meal and shares his faith in Christ.

No one can apply all the techniques that others have used in taking their stand for Jesus Christ. Find the method that best fits your personality and business and do it. Approximately 300,000 businesses in America are either owned or managed by Christians. Many believe that if revival is to come to our nation, it will be through these companies.

To take such a stand for Christ requires a total surrender of self and a willingness to accept ridicule from those who hate the things of God. But that's really no different from the way it has always been.

In order to be used by God we must first be willing to die for Him. As the apostle Paul says, *"But whatever things were gain to me, those things I have counted as loss for the sake of Christ. More than that, I count all things to be loss in view of the surpassing value of knowing Christ Jesus my Lord, for whom I have suffered the loss of all things, and count them but rubbish in order that I may gain Christ"* (Philippians 3:7-8).

The real question is, do you believe that? Or do you just say you believe it?

Notes

1. Finishing Strong, Steve Farrar, 1995, Multnomah Books.
2. Dear Abba, Claire Cloninger, 1997, Word Publishing.
3. Patton's Principles; For Managers Who Really Mean It, Porter B. Williamson, 1975, Touchstone Books, New York.

EXECUTIVE SUMMARY – CHAPTER 8

1. God encourages us to plan in our personal lives and businesses.

2. We must exercise the basic spiritual disciplines of prayer, reading the Bible, and spending time with other Christians to grow in Christ.

3. It is very important for Christian business people to meet regularly with other Christians in business to encourage one another and grow in their understanding of how to integrate faith and business excellence.

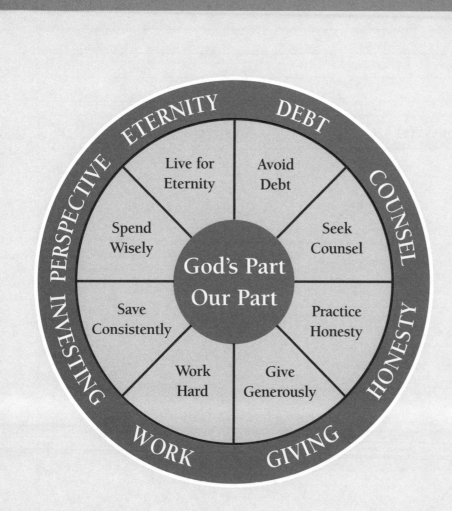

Be Faithful in Prayer

"Pray for one another. . . . The effective prayer of a righteous man can accomplish much"
(James 5:16).

"Pray for one another" (JAMES 5:16).

Name _____ Spouse _____

Home phone _____ Children (ages) _____

Business phone _____ _____

Cell phone _____ _____

E-mail _____ _____

Home address _____ _____

_____ _____

WEEK	PRAYER REQUEST(S)	ANSWERS TO PRAYER
1		
2		
3		
4		
5		
6		
7		
8	My long-term prayer request:	

PRAYER LOG

"Pray for one another" (James 5:16).

Name _____   Spouse _____

Home phone _____   Children (ages) _____

Business phone _____   _____

Cell phone _____   _____

E-mail _____   _____

Home address _____   _____

_____   _____

WEEK	PRAYER REQUEST(S)	ANSWERS TO PRAYER
1		
2		
3		
4		
5		
6		
7		
8	My long-term prayer request:	

PRAYER LOG

"Pray for one another" (JAMES 5:16).

Name _____   Spouse _____

Home phone _____   Children (ages) _____

Business phone _____   _____

Cell phone _____   _____

E-mail _____   _____

Home address _____   _____

_____   _____

WEEK	PRAYER REQUEST(S)	ANSWERS TO PRAYER
1		
2		
3		
4		
5		
6		
7		
8	My long-term prayer request:	

PRAYER LOG

"Pray for one another" (JAMES 5:16).

Name _____   Spouse _____

Home phone _____   Children (ages) _____

Business phone _____   _____

Cell phone _____   _____

E-mail _____   _____

Home address_____   _____

_____   _____

WEEK	PRAYER REQUEST(S)	ANSWERS TO PRAYER
1		
2		
3		
4		
5		
6		
7		
8	My long-term prayer request:	

PRAYER LOG

"Pray for one another" (JAMES 5:16).

Name _____   Spouse _____
Home phone _____   Children (ages) _____
Business phone _____   _____
Cell phone _____   _____
E-mail _____   _____
Home address _____   _____
_____   _____

WEEK	PRAYER REQUEST(S)	ANSWERS TO PRAYER
1		
2		
3		
4		
5		
6		
7		
8	My long-term prayer request:	

PRAYER LOG

"Pray for one another" (JAMES 5:16).

Name _____ Spouse _____

Home phone _____ Children (ages) _____

Business phone _____ _____

Cell phone _____ _____

E-mail _____ _____

Home address _____ _____

_____ _____

WEEK	PRAYER REQUEST(S)	ANSWERS TO PRAYER
1		
2		
3		
4		
5		
6		
7		
8	My long-term prayer request:	

"Pray for one another" (JAMES 5:16).

Name _____   Spouse _____

Home phone _____   Children (ages) _____

Business phone _____   _____

Cell phone _____   _____

E-mail _____   _____

Home address_____   _____

_____   _____

WEEK	PRAYER REQUEST(S)	ANSWERS TO PRAYER
1		
2		
3		
4		
5		
6		
7		
8	My long-term prayer request:	

PRAYER LOG

"Pray for one another" (JAMES 5:16).

Name _____   Spouse _____

Home phone _____   Children (ages) _____

Business phone _____   _____

Cell phone _____   _____

E-mail _____   _____

Home address _____   _____

_____   _____

WEEK	PRAYER REQUEST(S)	ANSWERS TO PRAYER
1		
2		
3		
4		
5		
6		
7		
8	My long-term prayer request:	

PRAYER LOG

INVOLVEMENT AND SUGGESTIONS

Date:_____

Please fill out both sides of this form. For your convenience, this form may be folded, sealed, and mailed to CROWN FINANCIAL MINISTRIES, postage paid (see the back of this form). To help save postage and processing costs, you may also complete this form online at **Crown.org/Business**.

Please Print

YOUR NAME ☐ MR ☐ MRS ☐ MS ☐ MISS ☐ DR ☐ REV

HOME ADDRESS

CITY   ST/PROV   ZIP/POSTAL CODE

COUNTRY

HOME PHONE   WORK PHONE

E-MAIL ADDRESS

NAME OF SMALL GROUP LEADER

NEWSLETTER AND E-MAIL

We send a weekly e-mail message and monthly newsletter sharing God's principles and communicating what the Lord is doing in CROWN FINANCIAL MINISTRIES. Please indicate below if you would like to receive these.

☐ Yes, I would like to like to receive CROWN'S weekly e-mail message.
☐ Yes, I would like to receive the monthly *Money Matters* newsletter.
☐ Yes, I would like to receive the monthly *Money Matters* newsletter by e-mail.

INVOLVEMENT

PRAY

☐ Yes, I would like to pray regularly for the Lord to expand CROWN and change lives through this ministry.

SERVE

Please send me information about:

☐ Becoming trained as a small group leader.
☐ Becoming trained as a budget counselor.
☐ Serving CROWN in my church.

SUPPORT

☐ Enclosed is a contribution to CROWN in the amount of $_____.
☐ I want to become a regular supporter of CROWN (a CROWN Outreach Partner). Enclosed is my first contribution in the amount of $_____.

Please tri-fold and seal. Do not staple.

1. Please indicate the most valuable part(s) of the study:
   - ❏ Scripture memorization
   - ❏ Prayer time
   - ❏ Fellowship with others
   - ❏ Learning God's financial principles
   - ❏ Budget and practical applications
   - ❏ Other: _____

2. Please indicate the most valuable session(s) of the study:
   - ❏ God's Part and Our Part
   - ❏ Debt
   - ❏ Counsel
   - ❏ Honesty
   - ❏ Giving
   - ❏ Work
   - ❏ Investing
   - ❏ Perspective and Contentment
   - ❏ Eternity
   - ❏ Other: _____

3. Please indicate all commitments you have made or will make as a result of the study:
   - ❏ Asked Jesus Christ to be my savior.
   - ❏ Committed to get out of debt.
   - ❏ Made plans to increase savings.
   - ❏ Other: _____
   - ❏ Train my children to be financially faithful.
   - ❏ Get a current will.
   - ❏ Increase giving to my church.
   - ❏ Other: _____

4. Do you have any suggestions for improving any areas?

   _____
   _____
   _____

5. We would appreciate your sharing what the Lord has done in your life through this study or any practical hints you have that would be especially helpful for other people.

   _____
   _____
   _____

PERSONAL INFORMATION

*Thank you for taking a moment to fill out the personal information form below. For your convenience, this form may be cut, folded, sealed, and mailed to Crown Financial Ministries postage paid (see guides on the back of this form). To help save postage and processing costs, you may also fill out this form online at **Crown.org/Business**.*   Date:_____

YOUR INFORMATION
Please Print

I AM A: ☐ STUDENT ☐ CO-LEADER ☐ LEADER   BUSINESS TITLE/OCCUPATION

YOUR TITLE: ☐ MR ☐ MRS ☐ MISS ☐ MS ☐ DR ☐ REV

YOUR FIRST NAME   YOUR LAST NAME

SPOUSE IS A: ☐ STUDENT ☐ CO-LEADER ☐ LEADER ☐ NONPARTICIPANT   BUSINESS TITLE/OCCUPATION

SPOUSE'S TITLE: ☐ MR ☐ MRS ☐ MISS ☐ MS ☐ DR ☐ REV

SPOUSE'S FIRST NAME   LAST NAME

YOUR HOME ADDRESS

CITY   ST/PROV   ZIP/POSTAL CODE

COUNTRY

HOME PHONE   WORK PHONE

E-MAIL ADDRESS

CHURCH INFORMATION

CHURCH NAME

CHURCH ADDRESS

CITY   ST/PROV   ZIP/POSTAL CODE

COUNTRY

LEADER INFORMATION

YOUR LEADER'S FIRST NAME   LAST NAME

CO-LEADER'S FIRST NAME   LAST NAME

BUSINESS REPLY MAIL
FIRST-CLASS MAIL   PERMIT NO 95   GAINESVILLE GA

POSTAGE WILL BE PAID BY ADDRESSEE

Crown Financial Ministries
PO Box 100
Gainesville GA 30503-9931

Please tri-fold and seal. Do not staple.

Fold here